SECOND EDITION

STEP FORWARD

**STANDARDS-BASED LANGUAGE LEARNING
FOR WORK AND ACADEMIC READINESS**

SERIES DIRECTOR
Jayme Adelson-Goldstein

Workbook

Renata Russo

OXFORD
UNIVERSITY PRESS

OXFORD
UNIVERSITY PRESS

198 Madison Avenue
New York, NY 10016 USA

Great Clarendon Street, Oxford, OX2 6DP, United Kingdom

Oxford University Press is a department of the University of Oxford.
It furthers the University's objective of excellence in research, scholarship,
and education by publishing worldwide. Oxford is a registered trade
mark of Oxford University Press in the UK and in certain other countries

ISBN: 978 0 19 449336 9 (WORKBOOK LEVEL 2)

Printed in China

This book is printed on paper from certified and well-managed sources

ACKNOWLEDGMENTS

Illustrations by: Kevin Brown/Top Dog Studios: 9, 16, 36, 38, 43, 44, 47, 48, 67, 78,
82; Susan Spellman: 2, 4, 30, 34, 54, 56, 61, 69, 79; Karen Minot: 12, 13, 21, 22,
27, 37, 41, 42, 45, 49, 50, 55, 56, 58, 70, 77, 84; Shawn Banner: 33, 52, 73, 77;
Laurie A. Conley: 6, 18, 32, 51, 59, 65. Rose Lowry: 2(second from left), 6, 30, 34.

*The publishers would like to thank the following for their kind permission to reproduce
photographs*: Cover, Click Bestsellers/Shutterstock.com; pg. 10 Chris Robbins/
Getty Images; pg. 14 vectorfusionart/Shutterstock; pg. 19 Risto0/Shutterstock,
Tutti Frutti/Shutterstock; pg. 24 iofoto/Shutterstock; pg. 25 Indeed/Getty
Images; pg. 28 Bernd Vogel/Getty Images; pg. 31 B.O'Kane/Alamy; pg. 35
Dave and Les Jacobs/Getty Images; pg. 36 Juice Images/Alamy; pg. 37 Marco
Rodrigues/Alamy Stock Photo, fizkes/Shutterstock, Bennian/Shutterstock,
Jupiterimages/Getty Images; pg. 39 Jeff Greenberg/Alamy Stock Photo, PM
Images/Getty Images, Jose Luis Pelaez Inc/Getty Images; pg. 42 kali9/Getty
Images; pg. 44 Donna Beeler/Shutterstock, Roman Samokhin/Shutterstock,
Julia_Lelija/Shutterstock, valigloo/Shutterstock, Andrii Gorulko/Shutterstock,
EugeniuNovac/Shutterstock, Tony Cordoza/Alamy Stock Photo, marilyn
barbone/Shutterstock, Mahathir Mohd Yasin/Shutterstock, qvist/Shutterstock;
pg. 46 Lev Dolgachov/Alamy, Dorling Kindersley/Getty Images, Trevor Pearson/
Alamy Stock Photo, Anthony Pleva/Alamy Stock Photo, fotomak/Shutterstock,
Binh Thanh Bui/Shutterstock; pg. 56 aabejon/Getty Images; pg. 62 Dmitry
Kalinovsky/Shutterstock; pg. 63 trolley/Alamy Stock Photo; pg. 68 Blend
Images - John Lund/Sam Diephuis/Getty Images; pg. 70 David A. Dobbs/Getty
Images; pg. 72 Mike Theiss/Getty Images, Mike Theiss/Contributor/Getty
Images, Ashley Cooper/Getty Images, Jon Beard/Shutterstock, Ammit Jack/
Shutterstock, Tainar/Shutterstock; pg. 75 Anton_Ivanov/Shutterstock

CONTENTS

A Match the pictures with the sentences.

_4_ David likes to look up words in the dictionary.

_5_ Kalila likes to copy new words in her notebook.

_3_ Dan likes to brainstorm ideas.

_1_ Mei likes to use a computer.

_2_ Terrell likes to listen to recordings.

B Complete the sentences. Use the words in the box.

| tablet | chart | group | flashcards | the Internet | pair |

1. Niki listens to English on her _____tablet_____.

2. Two students are working together. That's a ___pair.___.

3. Beth often uses the computer and works on _the Internet._.

4. There are three students in that ___group_____.

5. Alex likes to use _flashcards_____ with a partner.

6. Lucas and Moy are making a ____chart_____ to brainstorm new words.

A Complete the paragraph. Use the words in the box.

use the computer	listen to	a good listener
a partner	on the Internet	copy new words

I like my English class a lot. Every day is different and fun. On Mondays and Wednesdays, we go to the lab to _____use the computer_____. I like to study
1
new things _____on the Internet_____. On Tuesdays, I practice with
2
_____a partner_____. My partner's name is Lisa. I learn from her too. On
3
Thursdays, we _____listen to_____ recordings in class. It helps me understand
4
the new words. I also like to _____copy new words_____ in my notebook. I am
5
_____a good listerner_____ in class. I like to listen to my classmates and my teacher.
6

B How do you practice English? Take the quiz. Check (✔) *yes* or *no*.

How Do You Practice English?

1 Do you like to practice with a partner?
☑ yes ☐ no

2 Do you read stories in English?
☑ yes ☐ no

3 Do you listen to recordings?
☐ yes ☐ no

4 Do you listen to TV and radio programs in English?
☑ yes ☐ no

5 Do you write letters in English?
☑ yes ☐ no

6 Do you look up words in the dictionary?
☑ yes ☐ no

7 Do you make charts?
☑ yes ☐ no

8 Do you talk with friends and classmates in English?
☑ yes ☐ no

LOOK AT YOUR ANSWERS: Did you answer . . .
yes to 1, 3, 4, and 8? You like to listen and speak.
yes to 2, 5, 6, and 7? You like to read and write.
yes to more than 6 questions? You practice in many different ways. That's great!
no to more than 6 questions? Try to practice English in more ways. It's fun!

LESSON **3** GRAMMAR

A **Complete the sentences. Use the verbs in parentheses.**

1. Carlos _____needs to study_____ grammar. (need, study)

2. Linda _____wants to work_____ at home. (want, work)

3. Maria and Monica _____like to study_____ at night. (like, study)

4. They _____need to use_____ the computer. (need, use)

5. I _____want to work_____ alone. (want, work)

B **Look at the pictures. Answer the questions. Write two sentences.**

1. Does Rosa like to study in the evening?

   Rosa doesn't like to study in the

   evening.

   She likes to study in the morning.

3. Does Yoshi like to study alone?

   No, Yoshi doesn't like

   to study alone.

   He likes to study alone.

2. Do they need to study the simple past?

   No, they need to study

   the simple Posent.

4. Does Fernando want to use a math book?

   No, Hes doesn't want

   To use a grammar

C Unscramble the questions.

1. like to study / What / you / do

   <u>What do you like to study?</u>

2. Brenda / How does / like to learn

   <u>How does Brenda like to learn?</u>

3. they / do / When / need to study

   <u>When do they need to study?</u>

4. Where / she / want to meet / does

   <u>Where does she want to meet?</u>

D Match the questions with the answers.

<u>d</u> 1. What does she like to study?

<u>a</u> 2. Where does he want to meet?

<u>c</u> 3. When do you need to study?

<u>b</u> 4. How does David want to study?

a. He wants to meet at the library.

b. He wants to study with a partner.

c. I need to study tonight.

d. She likes to study grammar.

E Complete the sentences. Circle a or b.

1. _____ you need to practice reading?

   (a.) Do

   b. Does

2. Yes, they <u>do</u>. They love to watch movies.

   a. don't

   b. do

3. <u>Does</u> he want to study at the library with us?

   a. Does

   b. Was

4. No, I <u>don't</u>. I don't live here.

   a. doesn't

   b. don't

5. <u>Do</u> they need to study together?

   a. Were

   b. Do

A Complete the conversation. Use the words in the box.

> Hi, everyone
> It's nice to meet
> your name
> How do you

Carlos: <u>Hi, everyone</u> . I want to introduce my friend, Nadim Ali.
1

Teresa: What's <u>your name</u> again?
2

Nadim: Nadim Ali.

Teresa: <u>Ho do you</u> spell your first name?
3

Nadim: N-A-D-I-M.

Teresa: <u>It's nice to meet</u> you, Nadim.
4

Nadim: Nice to meet you too.

B Complete the conversation.

Vashon: Hi, I'm Vashon Evans.

Wendy: I'm sorry. <u>What's your name</u> again?
1

Vashon: Vashon.

Wendy: How <u>do you</u> your first name?
2

Vashon: V-A-S-H-O-N. What's your name?

Wendy: My name is Wendy Chow.

Vashon: How <u>do you</u> your last name?
3

Wendy: C-H-O-W.

Vashon: Oh. Nice to meet you.

Wendy: Nice <u>to meet you</u> too.
4

Vashon: Wendy, this is my friend Aaron Jones.

Wendy: <u>How do you</u> Aaron? A-A-R-O-N?
5

Aaron: Yes, <u>nice to meet you</u>.
6

Wendy: Nice to meet you too.

DO THE MATH Go to page 86.

A Read the course listing. How many classes are there?

Adult Education Courses – Fall Semester

Title	Dates	Days	Time	Location	Teacher	Cost
GED Science	8/20–12/14	M/W	9:00 a.m.–12:00 p.m.	C–18	Mr. Smith	$110
GED Math	8/20–12/14	M/W	1:00 p.m.–4:00 p.m.	C–16	Ms. Monroe	$130
GED Reading	8/14–12/6	T/Th	9:00 a.m.–12:00 p.m.	B–12	Ms. Campbell	$110
GED Writing	8/14–12/6	T/Th	1:00 p.m.–4:00 p.m.	B–14	Mr. Bell	$140

B Answer the questions. Use complete sentences.

1. Which classes are in the morning?

   GED Science and GED Reading are in the morning.

2. Which classes are in the afternoon?

   GED Math and GED writing

3. How much does Ms. Monroe's class cost?

   the class cost it is $130

4. Which days of the week does Mr. Smith's class meet?

   the days Monday and wemes'day

5. Where is Ms. Campbell's class?

   _____

6. When does Mr. Bell's class end?

   December 6

C What about you? Which class or classes do you want to take to improve your skills?

1. _____

2. _____

A Find the words in the puzzle. Circle them.

flashcards	practice	chart	resume	certificate
education	next	goal	degree	brainstorm

C	V	G	O	A	L	U	L	I	K	B	T	V
E	Y	N	U	L	I	D	E	G	R	E	E	F
R	M	I	L	O	P	T	E	W	A	Z	X	L
T	G	E	N	T	P	N	E	X	T	E	M	A
I	I	D	U	H	K	N	F	R	I	D	G	S
F	N	U	H	I	F	C	H	A	R	T	Z	H
I	Z	C	W	X	C	A	B	N	E	A	K	C
C	L	A	N	X	L	R	G	R	S	D	E	A
A	Y	T	B	X	J	S	D	E	U	F	T	R
T	B	I	J	N	T	E	U	U	M	N	V	D
E	R	O	N	X	Y	P	T	E	E	O	I	S
B	S	N	B	R	A	I	N	S	T	O	R	M
P	R	A	C	T	I	C	E	W	E	X	R	T

B Complete the sentences. Use the words in the puzzle.

1. I like to _____practice_____ vocabulary words with _flashcards_.

2. They're making a _brainstorm_ with new words.

3. Do you like to _practice_ new ideas with your classmates?

4. I want to learn a new language. That's my _____.

5. I want to get an Associate's _certificate_ to be a nurse.

6. He is studying to get a GED _certificate_.

7. She needs to prepare her _resume_ to apply for a new job.

8. First, he wants to get a good _____. _____, he wants to find a job that pays well.

A Complete the sentences. Circle *a* or *b*.

1. I'm ____. There's nothing to do here.

   a. energetic

   b. bored *(circled)*

2. Steve is very tired. He's ____.

   a. sleepy *(circled)*

   b. energetic

3. Mei gives Alison some flowers for her birthday. Alison is ____.

   a. upset

   b. surprised *(circled)*

4. The students are all late for class today. The teacher is ____.

   a. bored *(circled)*

   b. upset

5. Fernando can't understand the new words. He's ____.

   a. happy

   b. frustrated *(circled)*

B Complete the sentences. Use the words in the box.

thunderstorm	snowstorm	freezing	~~foggy~~	icy	warm

handwritten: Nevada   congelado

1. I can't see the house across the street. It's very ___foggy___.

2. Be careful! Don't fall. The streets are ___thunderstom___ today.

3. Look at the lightning! This is a bad ___snow storm___.

4. It's cold and cloudy today. We're going to have a ___icy___.

5. It's often humid in the summer. It's ___warm___, too.

6. Brr! It's ___freezing___ outside today. I'm wearing my winter coat.

A **Complete the paragraph. Use the words in the box.**

| his vacation | some friends | cool and sunny |
| ~~favorite season~~ | beautiful fall days | to go for walks |

Theo's _____favorite season_____ is fall.
1

He likes the __to go for walks.__ .
2

The weather is usually __his vacation.__ .
3

Fall is a good time for sports. Theo and his friends often play basketball

in the park. He also likes __beautiful fall days.__ .
4

He usually takes __his vacation__ in October.
5

This year, he will visit __some friends__ in Colorado.
6

B **Read the calendar. Answer the questions. Use complete sentences.**

October

Sun.	Mon.	Tues.	Wed.	Thurs.	Fri.	Sat.
1 music festival	2	3	4	5	6	7 farmers' market
8	9 Theo's vacation begins	10	11	12	13	14 basketball game

1. When is the music festival?

   It's on Sunday, October 1st.

2. When is the basketball game?

   It's on saturday, october 14.

3. When is the first day of Theo's vacation?

   It's on monday, October 9.

4. When is the farmers' market?

   It's on saturday, october 7.

will (auxiliar
will (para el futuro)
Ire.

A **Complete the sentences. Use *will* or *won't* and the verbs in parentheses.** *tu aprenderas*
you will learn

1. The concert _____will start_____ at 9:00 p.m. (start)
2. They _____won't go_____ to the movies with me. (not/go)
3. We _____will see_____ them at the party in July. (see)
4. She _____will be_____ on vacation in January. (be)
5. He _____will visit_____ his family in California in November. (visit)
6. The concert _____won't end_____ before 10 p.m. (not/end)

B **Read Walter's calendar. These sentences are false. Write the correct information.**

1. Walter will start school in February.

   Walter won't start school in February.

   He'll start school in March.

2. Walter will go to his brother's graduation in March.

   He'll go to brother's in April.

   _____

3. Walter will visit his parents in January.

   He'll visit parents in february.

   _____

4. Walter will go on vacation in April.

   He'll go on vacation in january.

   _____

January
go on vacation

February
visit parents

March
start school

April
go to brother's
graduation

C **Match the questions with the answers.**

_e_ 1. When will they be back?

_c_ 2. When will Julia start school?

_d_ 3. When will we be on vacation?

_b_ 4. When will he go for a walk?

_a_ 5. Where will you be at this time tomorrow?

a. I'll be at work.

b. He'll go for a walk tomorrow.

c. She'll start school in September.

d. We'll be on vacation in July.

e. They'll be back in May.

D **Answer the questions. Circle *a* or *b*.**

1. When will she start school?
   a. She'll start school in the fall. *(circled)*
   b. Yes, she will.

2. Will they go to the concert?
   a. It'll start at 5:00 p.m.
   b. Yes, they will.

3. When will Peter go on vacation?
   a. He'll go in December.
   b. No, he won't.

4. Where will you be at this time next week?
   a. I am at work.
   b. I'll be at work.

5. Where will they be five years from now?
   a. They're in New York.
   b. They'll be in New York.

E **Read the notes. Write sentences with *will* or *won't*.**

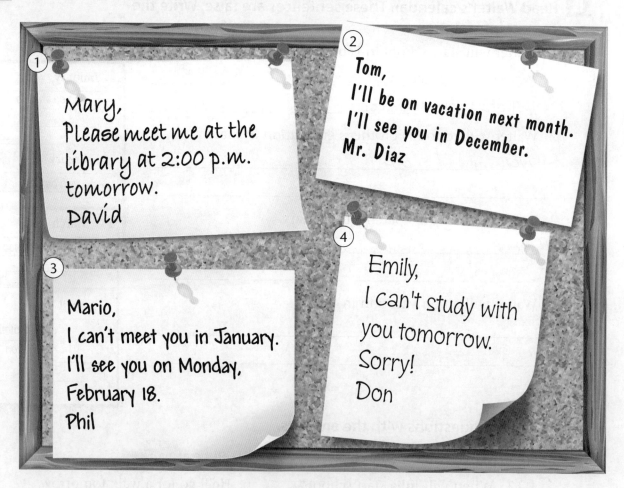

1. Mary,
   Please meet me at the library at 2:00 p.m. tomorrow.
   David

2. Tom,
   I'll be on vacation next month. I'll see you in December.
   Mr. Diaz

3. Mario,
   I can't meet you in January. I'll see you on Monday, February 18.
   Phil

4. Emily,
   I can't study with you tomorrow. Sorry!
   Don

1. David will meet Mary at the library tomorrow at 2:00 p.m.
2. _____
3. _____
4. _____

Look at the map. Complete the conversation. Use the words in the box.

Go up	the bridge	~~How can I get~~	Go straight
that's it	turn right	next to	go past the bank

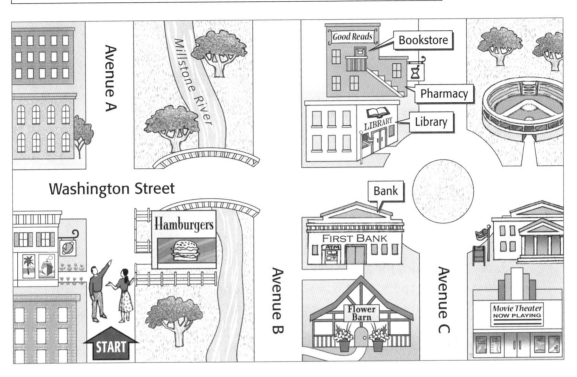

A: Excuse me. _____How can I get_____ to the library?

                                1

B: _____ on Avenue A. Then _____ and

                  2   3

go over the bridge.

A: Go over _____?

                            4

B: Yes, _____. The library is on the left

                    5

_____ the pharmacy.

             6

A: Oh, and is there a bookstore near here?

B: Yes, it's above the pharmacy. _____ the steps on the left.

                                          7

A: And is there a movie theater near here?

B: Yes, after you go over the bridge, _____ and turn right on

                                              8

Avenue C. The movie theater is on your left.

A: Thank you.

B: You're welcome.

A Read the article. What can you do to make small talk easier?

How To Make Small Talk

Do you feel nervous with strangers? Is it difficult to talk to people you don't know? Here are some ideas that will make small talk easier for you.

1. Practice.
  • Talk with everyone: neighbors, classmates, restaurant servers, children, everyone!
  • Be a good listener. You don't have to talk all the time!
2. Have good topics for small talk.
  • Read newspapers, magazines, books, signs, everything.
  • Try something new! Play a new sport. Eat a different food.

Do these things, and you will have a lot to talk about!

B Complete the sentences. Circle *a* or *b*.

1. Some people feel _____ with large groups.

   a. difficult   (b.) nervous

2. The article has _____ ideas to make small talk easy.

   (a.) one   b. two

3. Talk with other people. Then small talk will be _____ for you.

   (a.) easier   b. more difficult

4. The article says you can get ideas for small talk from _____.

   (a.) books and newspapers   b. your homework

5. To have small talk topics, it's important to _____.

   (a.) do the same things   b. try something new

UNIT 2 ANOTHER LOOK

Complete the sentences. Use the words in the box. Then complete the puzzle.

weather	frustrated	vacation	icy	Thunderstorms
festival	mood	bored	cool	~~over~~

Humor

Across

1. Go _____ over _____ the bridge on First Street.

4. This book isn't interesting. I'm _____.

6. Be careful! The sidewalk is _____.

8. Do you want to go to the music _____?

9. Look at the lightning! _____ can be dangerous.

10. Are you in the _____ for conversation?

Down

2. Steve will go to Hawaii on _____ in December.

3. He's very _____. His car won't start.

5. It's _____ in here. I need a sweater.

7. The _____ will be warm and humid tomorrow.

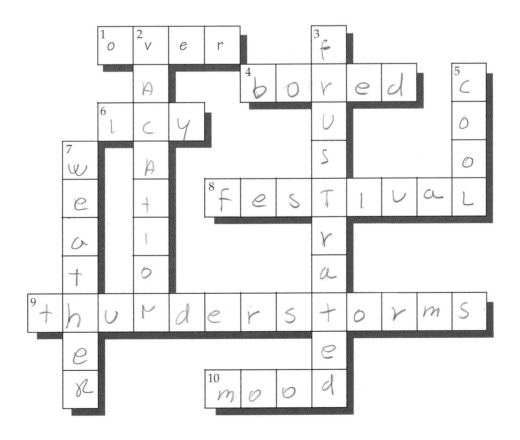

A **Match the words with the pictures. Use the words in the box.**

leaking pipe	no electricity	~~cracked window~~
mice	dripping faucet	broken door

1. <u>cracked window</u>

2. _____

3. _____

4. _____

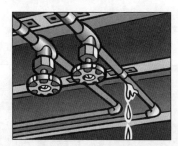

5. _____

6. _____

B **Match the problems with the solutions.**

<u>f</u> 1. There's a cracked window in the bedroom.

____ 2. There's no electricity in the basement.

____ 3. There's a leaking pipe in the bathroom.

____ 4. I can't find my key.

____ 5. There are cockroaches in the garage.

____ 6. There's a broken door in the living room.

a. What is the locksmith's phone number?

b. The plumber will be here soon.

c. The electrician will check the fuse box.

d. Let's call the carpenter.

e. We need to call the exterminator.

f. The repair person will fix it.

A Complete the paragraph. Use the words in the box.

safe neighborhood	There is also	four bathrooms	~~small house~~
for their children	living room	have a big family	three bedrooms

Mr. and Mrs. Smith live in a _____small house_____.
                                          1

They _____ with six children! There are _____
              2   3

and two bathrooms in the house. _____ a small office in the house.
                                                          4

The Smiths are looking for their dream house. They want a bigger house

_____. Their dream house has five bedrooms and
          5

_____. They want a very large _____ for the
          6   7

family to watch TV together. They want a house in a _____ so their
                                                                          8

children can play outside.

B Read the ads. Mark the sentences *T* (true) or *F* (false).

(A) **Apartment for rent**

1BR/1BA apt, 1st floor, nr school
$600/mo. $250 sec. dep.
Call mgr at (250) 555-3000

(B) **Apartment for rent**

Lg 2BR/1BA apt, 3rd floor
$700/mo. $300 sec. dep.
Call mgr at (250) 555-6363

__F__ 1. Apartment A has two bedrooms.

_____ 2. The rent for apartment B is $700 a month.

_____ 3. There is a $250 security deposit for apartment A.

_____ 4. Apartment B is a small apartment.

_____ 5. There is no security deposit for apartment B.

_____ 6. Apartment A is on the 3rd floor.

A Complete the chart.

Adjective	Comparative
1. safe	safer
2. dangerous	more dangerous
3. small	
4. good	
5. convenient	
6. dark	
7. expensive	
8. sunny	
9. large	
10. bad	

B Look at the pictures. Write sentences about the two apartments. Use the comparative form of the adjectives in parentheses.

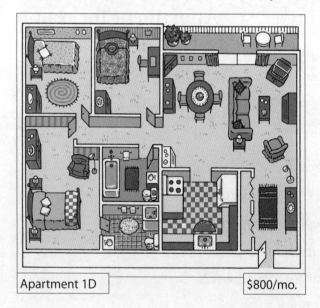

Apartment 1D $800/mo.

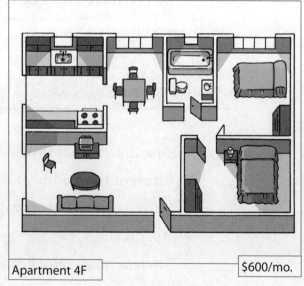

Apartment 4F $600/mo.

1. <u>Apartment 4F is sunnier than apartment 1D.</u> _____ (sunny)
2. _____ (expensive)
3. _____ (large)
4. _____ (cheap)
5. _____ (small)

C Complete the questions. Use the comparative. Then answer with your opinion.

1. Which is _colder, the house or the cabin_____?
   (cold)
   _I think the cabin is colder than the house_____.

2. Which is _____?
   (sunny)
   _____.

3. Which is _____?
   (big)
   _____.

log cabin

4. Which is _____?
   (pretty)
   _____.

5. Which is _____?
   (comfortable)
   _____.

6. Which is _____?
   (expensive)
   _____.

adobe house

D Complete the sentences using an adverb of degree. Use *much, a lot, a little,* or *a bit*. Answers may vary.

1. This house is ____much____ larger than the one-bedroom apartment we rented last year.

2. That large office building is _____ more expensive than my small house.

3. We are moving to save $50.00 a month. Our new apartment is _____ cheaper than the old one.

4. Boston is _____ colder than Miami in the winter.

5. My new house is only _____ bigger than my old apartment. It has an extra bathroom.

6. A big house is _____ more comfortable than a small apartment.

7. A neighborhood in a small city is _____ quieter than in a big city.

8. Andy and Mary are almost the same height. Andy is _____ taller than Mary.

A Read the ad. Complete the conversation.

Brian: Hey, Karen. Here's an apartment for rent.

Karen: Oh, really? How much is it?

Brian: It's _____$700 a month_____.
        1

Karen: That's a little expensive. How many bedrooms does the apartment have?

Brian: It has _____.
        2
The apartment is on the _____ floor.
                3

Karen: Is there a _____?
        4

Brian: Yes, the security deposit is _____.
                5

Karen: That sounds great! Let's see it.

Apartment for rent

Lg 2BR/2BA apt 1st floor nr sch
$700/mo. $350 sec. dep., utils. incl.
Call mgr at (205) 555-2221

B Match the questions with the answers.

_c_ 1. How many bedrooms does the house have?

____ 2. Is there a security deposit?

____ 3. How much is the rent?

____ 4. Are utilities included?

____ 5. When is the apartment available?

____ 6. Is there parking?

a. It's available next month.

b. It's $850 a month.

c. It has three bedrooms.

d. Yes, there are two spaces.

e. Yes, it's $500.

f. No, they're not.

C Complete the conversation. Ask questions about apartment regulations.

Betty: Hello. _____Can I have a party?_____
                1

Manager: Yes, you can, but no loud music after 10:00 p.m.

Betty: _____?
                2

Manager: Yes, pets are allowed.

Betty: _____?
                3

Manager: No smoking is allowed in the backyard.

Betty: Thank you.

DO THE MATH Go to page 87.

A Read the article. What is one way to save money when renting an apartment?

C ← → 🔍 http://www.savemoneyrenting.org ≡

How to save money when renting an apartment

Renting an apartment can be expensive. Here are three ways to save money.

1. **Rent an apartment with a roommate.** You can ask friends, co-workers, classmates, or family members who are also looking for an apartment to be your roommate. It is much cheaper to share the rent and utilities with someone else than to rent by yourself.

2. **Pay attention to rental agreement details.** Always read rental agreements carefully. Parking and storage fees can be included in the agreement. Sometimes you can get one or two months of free rent when you sign for one year or longer. Talk to the landlord before signing an agreement that might cost you extra.

3. **Reduce your utility costs.** There are many landlords who will include your utilities in the rent. Again, make sure to look on the Internet and check your local newspaper for these options before signing a rental agreement.

B Answer the questions. Use complete sentences.

1. What is the main topic of the article?

   The main topic of the article is how to save money when renting an apartment.

2. What does the article say about finding a roommate?

   _____

3. Is it cheaper to rent an apartment with a roommate or by yourself?

   _____

4. Why should you read rental agreements carefully?

   _____

5. How can you reduce your utility costs?

   _____

C Answer the questions about yourself.

1. Do you prefer to rent by yourself or to have a roommate?

2. What are some other ways you can reduce your utility costs?

Unscramble the words.

Household Problems

kcercad niwwod *cracked window*

rbenko odro _____

cime _____

on leecytirict _____

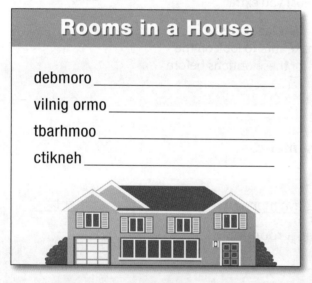

Repair People

cklomsthi _____

mbrepul _____

roexmitatren _____

ncateieclir _____

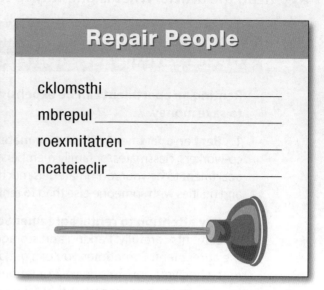

Rooms in a House

debmoro _____

vilnig ormo _____

tbarhmoo _____

ctikneh _____

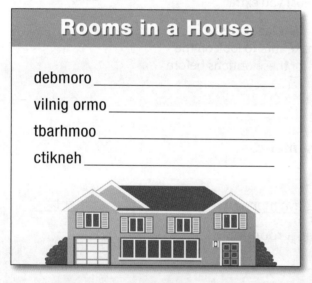

Places to Live

gbi tyci _____

lmals onwt _____

rlgae uhoes _____

nsuny ptaratmne _____

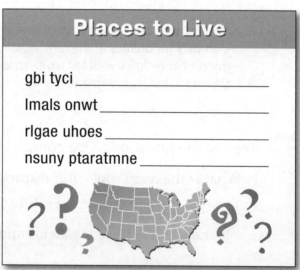

Rental Agreements

iuisitelt _____

tnre _____

netatn _____

ireucyst stiepdo _____

Apartment Searches

leartn cgayen _____

swaprenpe _____

etreintn _____

LESSON 1 VOCABULARY

A Read the job application. Write the names of the sections. Use the words in the box.

| Employment history | Job skills | References | Education | ~~Personal information~~ |

APPLICATION FOR EMPLOYMENT

1. Personal Information

Name: (last, first, middle initial)
Hernandez, Carla M

Address: (street, city, state)
301 Melo Road
San Jose, CA

Telephone: (901) 555-0102

2. Education

Name of institution: (dates)
WRC Community College: 2012–2014

3. Employment history

Jobs: (position, employer, dates)
Assistant manager, Lee's Supermarket, 2012–present
Cashier, Lee's Supermarket, 2010–2012

4. Job skills

Languages:
English, Spanish, Italian
Can you use a computer? (yes) no

5. References

(name, contact information)
Paul Lee, employer, (901) 555-3967
Gloria Vega, teacher, (901) 555-2843

B Who says these things? Match the sentences with the jobs.

_c_ 1. I deliver letters to people every day.

_a_ 2. Do you need some help with your taxes?

_b_ 3. I love to work with animals.

_c_ 4. What size jacket do you need?

a. sales clerk

b. veterinarian

c. mail carrier

d. accountant

A Complete the paragraph. Use the words in the box.

be nervous	job interviews	~~job skills~~	a suit and tie
the interviewer	make eye contact	on time	write questions

Rosa teaches a _____ job skills _____ class.
Here are some of the tips she gives her students
about _____ write questions _____.
1

2

• Before the interview, _____ be nervous _____
3
to ask the interviewer.

• Be _____ on time _____ for the interview. Don't be late!
4

• Men should wear _____ a suit and tie _____. Women should wear a suit,
5
with nice pants or a skirt.

• Smile and say hello to _____ make eye contact _____.
6

• You should _____ job interviews _____ when you shake hands.
7

• Finally, don't _____ the interviewer _____!
8

Follow these simple rules that Rosa gives her students, and you'll get the job!

B Read the job ad. Complete the sentences. Use complete words, not abbreviations.

> ### Accountant
>
> P/T, five yrs. accounting exp. req.
> Email employment history and refs. to
> lora4892@bcc.com. No phone calls please.
> Start immed. Billy Craig Company

1. The Billy Craig Company needs an _____ accountant _____.

2. The job is _____ five yrs. _____, not full-time.

3. Five years of accounting _____ exp _____ is _____ req _____ for this job.

4. You need to email your employment history and _____ refs _____ to
lora4892@bcc.com.

5. The job starts _____ immed. _____.

A Complete the sentences. Use the simple past of the verbs in parentheses.

1. Last night, our family ____ate____ dinner together. (eat)

2. At the table, we __talked__ about our day. (talk)

3. Our son __got__ a good grade on his English test yesterday. (get)

4. My husband __went__ to a Spanish class after work. (go)

5. Our daughter __applyed__ for a job at the supermarket today. (apply)

6. After dinner, I __wrote__ a letter to my friends in Miami. (write)

B Complete the sentences. Then write negative sentences. Use the simple past and words in parentheses.

1. We ____took____ Italian classes in January and February. (take)

   _We didn't take Spanish classes._____ (Spanish)

2. Alicia ____had____ a job interview at the post office yesterday. (have)

   _She_____ (bank)

3. Steve _____ at the National Bank for six months. (work)

   _____ (Roy's Supermarket)

4. Melissa _____ a job at the supermarket. (get)

   _____ (post office)

5. Jon _____ from nursing school in 2014. (graduate)

   _____ (in 2013)

6. I _____ two books in July. (read)

   _____ (the newspaper)

C Read the job applications. Unscramble the information questions. Then write the answers. Use the simple past.

JOB APPLICATION

<u>Personal Information</u>

Name:

Keisha Washington

Employment history:

Accountant: State Bank (from 2008 to 2014)

JOB APPLICATION

<u>Personal Information</u>

Name:

Gao Wang

Education:

B.A. University of California (2010)

Employment history:

Teacher: Lewis Elementary School (from 2010 to 2016)

1. Keisha / work / did / Where

   A: <u>Where did Keisha work</u> ?

   B: <u>Keisha worked at a bank</u> .

2. work / How long / Keisha / State Bank / at / did

   A: _____ ?

   B: _____ .

3. Gao / the University of California / did / graduate from / When

   A: _____ ?

   B: _____ .

4. Gao / work at / did / Lewis Elementary School / How long

   A: _____ ?

   B: _____ .

D Write information questions with the simple past of the verbs in the chart.

Column 1	Column 2	Column 3	Column 4
~~What time~~	she	~~get home~~	~~yesterday~~
How long	they	study	English
Where	~~you~~	go	to school
When	he	take	Spanish classes

1. <u>What time did you get home yesterday?</u>

2. _____ ?

3. _____ ?

4. _____ ?

A Read John's job application. Then complete the conversation.

Application for Employment	
Name: John Smith	
Experience: 2 years as an office manager at BZD, Inc.	**Education:** Bachelor's degree in computer science
Special skills: computers, good at working with people	**Reference:** Carla Santiago, President of BZD, Inc.

Interviewer: Tell me about your education.

John: I have a _____bachelor's_____ degree in _____.
                                1   2

Interviewer: How much experience do you have?

John: I worked for _____ years as an _____.
                                      3   4

Interviewer: Do you have any special skills?

John: I'm good at _____ and working _____.
                                      5   6

Interviewer: Do you have any references?

John: Yes, I do. _____ will give me a reference. She's the
                                        7

        president of BZD, Inc.

B Complete the sentences. Use adverbs of manner.

1. She writes ____slowly____. (slow)

2. They drive _____. (careful)

3. Tony works _____. (quick)

4. You are an excellent writer. You write very _____. (good)

5. I left the bedroom _____ because the baby was sleeping. (quiet)

6. Our team lost the game last night. They played very _____. (bad)

DO THE MATH Go to page 88.

A Read about John's career. What is his job?

Planning for Success

John Fernandez graduated with a bachelor's degree in computer science in 2003. After five years as an office assistant, John accepted a job as a computer programmer at a different company. The salary was much better, but John had to work on weekends.

John decided to make a change because he was tired of working so much. He went to see a job counselor for some advice. The counselor told him to make a plan to change his career. The plan included:

1. Decide on a new career.
2. Take some classes to learn new skills.
3. Revise his resume for his new career.

John is excited about his new plan. He hopes to make his decision about a new career very soon.

B Read the questions. Circle *a*, *b*, or *c*.

1. What was John's first job after he graduated?

   a. computer programmer

   b. office assistant

   c. teacher

2. Why did John accept a job as a computer programmer?

   a. because he wanted to work at a different company

   b. because he wanted to work on weekends

   c. because the salary was much better

3. Why did John decide to make a career change?

   a. because he loved his job

   b. because he was tired of working so much

   c. because of the job counselor's advice

4. What does the career plan include?

   a. learning new skills

   b. asking for advice

   c. being excited

Kate wants to apply for a new job. She has education and work experience. But Kate is not very organized! Help Kate complete this job application. Use her notes to help.

- I can use computers.
- Simms' Restaurant Service 2014–present
- Jennifer's phone number: (303) 555-2134

State – Bachelor's degree 2012–2014

Assistant Manager, Flynn's Restaurant 2012–2014

From: kate@internet.us
To: ewilson52@net.us
Subject: New Apartment!

Hi Mom,
My new apartment is great! Here's my new address and phone number: 2121 Post Street, Denver, Colorado 80202, (303) 555-7750. I'll see you soon!
Love,
Kate

- Languages: English, Spanish

City Community College, 2010–2012 associate degree Denver

JOB APPLICATION

Personal Information

NAME (LAST/FIRST)			
Wilson, Kate			

ADDRESS (NUMBER/STREET)	(CITY)	(CITY/STATE)
		Colorado

TELEPHONE (DAY)	(EVENING)
(303) 555-6520	

EMAIL
kate@internet.us

Employment History (Start with most recent job)

EMPLOYER 1 (NAME)	(POSITION)	(DATES)	(CITY/STATE)
	Manager		Denver, Colorado
EMPLOYER 2 (NAME)	(POSITION)	(DATES)	(CITY/STATE)
		2012–2014	Denver, Colorado

Education (Start with most recent)

SCHOOL 1 (NAME)	(DEGREE)	(DATES)	(CITY/STATE)
State University			Denver, Colorado
SCHOOL 2 (NAME)	(DEGREE)	(DATES)	(CITY/STATE)
	associate degree		

Job Skills

COMPUTER SKILLS	LANGUAGES
☐ YES ☐ NO	

Reference

NAME	CONTACT INFORMATION
Jennifer Long	

5 On the Job

LESSON 1 VOCABULARY

A **Complete the chart. Use the words in the box.**

hourly rate	~~gross pay~~	net pay
federal tax	Social Security	pay period

Kinds of pay	Deductions	Earnings
gross pay		

B **Look at the picture. Check (✓) what you see.**

- ✓ printer
- ____ keyboard
- ____ photocopier
- ____ file cabinet
- ____ monitor
- ____ hand cart
- ____ time clock
- ____ water cooler

C **Look at the picture in B. Complete the questions.**

1. **A:** Where is the _____printer_____?
   B: It's on the desk.

2. **A:** Where is the _____?
   B: It's next to the window.

3. **A:** Where is the _____?
   B: It's to the right of the printer.

4. **A:** Where is the _____?
   B: It's next to the file cabinet.

A Complete the paragraphs. Use the words in the box.

the deductions	~~rules~~	on time	a uniform
time clock	net pay	pay period	needs to

Samir works as a cashier at a supermarket. In his first week,

he learned some _____rules_____. He has to be
                          1

_____, and he has to wear _____.
         2   3
Samir also _____ smile at the customers.
                    4
Finally, every morning Samir needs to put his time card in the

_____.
         5

The _____ is seven days. Samir always looks carefully at
              6

_____ and his _____.
         7   8

Samir works a lot. He needs money to go to college next year.

B Where is this behavior appropriate? Check (✓) *Work, School,* or *Both* in the chart.

Behavior	Work	School	Both
1. Wear a hard hat	✓		
2. Don't be late			
3. Wear appropriate clothing			
4. Ask the teacher for help			
5. Be nice to customers			
6. No drinks near computers			

A **Unscramble the sentences. Then write the negative.**

1. have an accident / might / He

   <u>He might have an accident.</u>

   <u>He might not have an accident.</u>

2. might / get hurt / She

   _____

   _____

3. be safe / might / I

   _____

   _____

4. see the sign / They / might

   _____

   _____

B **Look at the pictures. Complete the sentences. Use _might_ or _might not_ and the verbs in parentheses.**

1. Marco _____<u>might ask</u>_____ his co-worker for help. (ask)

2. Steve _____ home early today. (go)

3. Marco _____ fired. (get)

4. Steve _____ a raise. (get)

5. Marco _____ his work on time. (finish)

6. Steve _____ his co-worker. (help)

C Linda starts a new job tomorrow. Complete the charts. Use *should* or *shouldn't* and the words in the box.

be late	~~complain about work~~	pay attention	go home early
be nervous	~~help her co-workers~~	ask questions	make eye contact

Things Linda should do

She should help her co-workers.

Things Linda shouldn't do

She shouldn't complain about work.

D Complete the paragraphs. Use *might (not)* or *should (not)*.

Joe is driving to work, and it's snowing. Joe ___shouldn't___ drive very fast.
                                                        1
He _____ have an accident. He _____ get to work on time, but his
            2   3
boss will understand.

Bernard is an electrician. He _____ wear safety gloves. His hands
                                      4
_____ get hurt on the job. Bernard _____ go to work without his
       5   6
uniform. His clothes _____ get dirty.
                           7

A Complete the conversation. Use the words in the box.

print these	make copies	right away
that letter	~~write an email~~	operate the forklift

Mr. Vega: Good morning, Scott. Could you

write an email to Paula, please? Ask her to
1

see me at 10 a.m.

Scott: I'll do it _____.
2

I can go the post office this morning.

Should I send _____ to Mr. Chow?
3

Mr. Vega: Yes, please. Could you also turn on the

printer and _____ documents?
4

Scott: Of course. Anything else?

Mr. Vega: Use the new photocopier, and _____ of these letters. Oh, and one
5

more thing. Tell Franco it's OK to _____ in the delivery area now.
6

Scott: No problem.

Mr. Vega: Well, that's all for now. Thank you.

B Write requests with *can* or *could*. Use the words in parentheses.

1. **A:** _Could you write an email to Maria, please?_____

   (write an email to Maria)
   B: Of course. What's Maria's email address?

2. **A:** John, _____

   (ask your sister to print the school letter)

   B: Sure, Dad. I'll ask her.

3. **A:** _____

   (type this letter)

   B: I'll do it right away.

4. **A:** _____

   (borrow your phone)

   B: Sure Mom. Here it is.

DO THE MATH Go to page 89.

A Read the article. What is one way you can get a good evaluation?

GET A GOOD PERFORMANCE EVALUATION

Here are some things you can do to get a good performance evaluation.

- *Show a positive attitude.* A negative attitude doesn't help anyone.
- *Don't complain about little things.* Maybe you can fix the problem. Talk to a co-worker and find a solution.
- *Be friendly to customers and co-workers.* Smile at customers. Don't be angry with co-workers.
- *Show that you want to learn new things.* For example, ask questions about the new computer. Try to use the printer.
- *Cooperate with co-workers.* Show that you want to work with co-workers.
- *Show that you are a hard worker.* Finish your work. Then help others.
- *Follow important safety and health rules.* Be sure you understand all the company rules.
- *Listen carefully to instructions.* Ask for help when you don't understand.
- *Be on time for work.* Don't be late. If you are sick, call your manager.

B Priya read the article above and then did everything right at work. Later she got a very good evaluation. Complete Priya's job evaluation.

Job Evaluation

Employee name: *Priya Singh*

1. __√__ Shows a positive attitude
   ____ Shows a negative attitude

2. ____ Complains often about little things
   ____ Doesn't complain about little things

3. ____ Wants to learn new things
   ____ Doesn't want to learn new things

4. ____ Is a hard worker
   ____ Is not a hard worker

5. ____ Follows important rules
   ____ Doesn't follow important rules

6. ____ Is late for work
   ____ Is on time for work

A Read about Rosie and complete the conversation. Use *can, could, should,* or *might.*

Rosie works as a sales clerk at an electronics store. She started her new job last week. She wants to do the best job she can, but she is worried she doesn't understand much about smart phones. Rosie decided to ask her teacher, Ms. Nguyen, for some help.

Rosie:	Hello, Ms. Nguyen. I'm calling because I'm worried about my new job.
Ms. Nguyen:	Hi, Rosie. I'm sorry to hear that. How _____can_____ I help you? 　　　　　　　1
Rosie:	Well, _____ you teach me a little bit about smart phones? I really 　　　　2 _____ know more for my job. 　3
Ms. Nguyen:	Smart phones? I _____ be able to help you with that. I have some 　　　　　　　4 experience using different smart phones.
Rosie:	Thank you very much. I _____ meet you tomorrow. 　　　　　　　　　5
Ms. Nguyen:	Great. I have a busy morning, but you _____ come in the 　　　　　　　　　　　　　　　　6 afternoon. How about 1 p.m.?
Rosie:	OK. See you then, Ms. Nguyen.

B Ali works in a construction site. Write three rules he should follow in the workplace. Use *should (not)* or *might (not).*

1. _____

2. _____

3. _____

LESSON 1 VOCABULARY

A **Look at the phone bill. Answer the questions.**

1. How many minutes did Monica spend on voice calls this month?

   Monica spent 1,010 minutes.

2. What are Monica's monthly data charges?

   _____

3. What are Monica's monthly service charges?

   _____

4. What is the total due on her bill?

   _____

HSNU**COMMUNICATIONS** 🌐)))
Monica Ruiz
(222) 555-1171
Bill Summary from 06/25/17–07/24/17
Voice Usage:
Mobile to Mobile – 448 minutes (unlimited)
Nights and Weekends – 562 minutes (unlimited)
Data Usage:
Used 2.8 GB
Remaining 0.2 GB

Monthly Data Charges:	$30.00
Monthly Service Charges:	$40.00
Total Due:	**$70.00**

B **Look at the pictures. Complete the sentences. Use the words in the box.**

getting a cab	checking her messages	~~using a headset~~
listening to a voice mail	using an app	using a cell phone
making an emergency call	~~leaving a message~~	

Hi, Mom. Call me back when you get this message.

Your cab will arrive in five minutes.

1. She's _____using a headset_____.

   She's _____leaving a message_____.

2. He's _____.

   He's _____.

Help! My house is on fire! I'm on the corner of East Avenue and Elm Street.

You have one new message. Beep. "Hi, Karen. It's your dad. Call me..."

3. He's _____.

   He's _____.

4. She's _____.

   She's _____.

LESSON 2 WRITING

A Complete the paragraphs about Tara. Use the words in the box.

| to get fired | a fever and sore throat | ~~to call in sick~~ |
| had to stay | was angry | sick child |

Tara works at a bank, and she has three children. She doesn't like ___to call in sick___,
1

but sometimes she needs to. When she has a _____, she has
2

to stay home.

Last month, Tara had _____. She felt terrible and called in sick for three
3

days. Then two of her children got sick. She _____ home for two more
4

days.

Tara's manager _____. There was a lot of work. Tara doesn't want
5

_____.
6

B Match the sentences with the pictures. Write the sentences.

| I feel terrible. I have a cold. | ~~I missed the bus.~~ |
| My child has a fever. | I overslept yesterday. |

1. I missed the bus._____

2. _____

3. _____

4. _____

A **Read the chart. Then add your own information.**

Ali and Fatima

Arnold

Rosa

	Right now	Every morning
Ali and Fatima	shop for food	have breakfast at 8:00 a.m.
Arnold	jog	read the newspaper
Rosa	make dinner	get up at 7:00 a.m.
My information		

B **Look at the chart in A. Complete the sentences. Use the present continuous and the simple present.**

1. Ali and Fatima _____*are shopping for food*_____ right now.

2. They _____ every morning.

3. Arnold _____ right now.

4. He _____ every morning.

5. Rosa _____ right now.

6. She _____ every morning.

C **Write about yourself. What are you doing right now? What do you do every morning? Use the present continuous and the simple present.**

1. _____

2. _____

3. _____

4. _____

D Complete the answers. Use the present continuous.

1. **A:** Is she sleeping at the moment?

    B: Yes, _she is sleeping_ at the moment.

2. **A:** Are they watching a movie right now?

    B: No, _____ right now.

3. **A:** Is he studying today?

    B: No, _____ today.

4. **A:** Are you texting right now?

    B: Yes, _____ right now.

E Match the questions with the answers.

_d_ 1. What are you doing?

____ 2. How often do you talk on the phone?

____ 3. Where are they living at the moment?

____ 4. How many hours does he study every night?

____ 5. When do they usually get home?

____ 6. What is he drinking right now?

a. I talk on the phone twice a day.

b. They usually get home at 7:00 p.m.

c. He is drinking some tea right now.

d. I am having dinner.

e. They are living in a small house at the moment.

f. He studies two hours every night.

F Complete the sentences. Use the present continuous or the simple present.

1. I _____am writing_____ an email to my teacher now. (write)

2. What _____are_____ you _____doing_____ at the park at the moment? (do)

3. Julie _____ for her test right now. (study)

4. How often _____ they _____ to England? (travel)

5. Please don't talk. We _____ a math test. (take)

6. What _____ she _____ for breakfast every morning? (eat)

7. Right now I _____ my brother. (call)

8. Where _____ they _____ for dinner every Friday night? (go)

A Complete the conversation. Use the words in the box.

May I take	~~can I help you~~	This is
speak to Mr. Gonzalez	give him the message	isn't in

Takeshi: Good morning, Good Food Restaurant.

How _can I help you_____?

1

Carlos: Hello. May I _____, please?

2

Takeshi: I'm sorry. He _____ today.

3

_____ a message?

4

Carlos: Yes. _____ Carlos Hernandez,

5

his accountant. Can you ask Mr. Gonzalez to call me, please? My number

is 555-4724.

Takeshi: OK. I'll _____ tomorrow.

6

Carlos: Thank you. Goodbye.

B Look at the conversation in A. Complete the telephone message.

While you were out...	
For:	
From:	
Message	

C Match the questions with the answers.

_c_ 1. How often do you talk on the phone?   a. They usually get home at 7:00 p.m.

____ 2. What is she doing right now?   b. No, he isn't.

____ 3. When do they usually get home?   c. I talk on the phone every day.

____ 4. Is he doing his homework at the moment?   d. She is reading a book right now.

DO THE MATH Go to page 89.

A Read the article. What is a retirement community?

Retirement Communities

Many Americans move to retirement[1] communities when they get older. A retirement community is a place for seniors to live, and it offers many different services. Counselors give seniors advice, and nurses care for their health. At social events, seniors can have fun and meet new people.

In retirement communities, there are usually volunteers. In their free time, volunteers help the seniors. For example, they go for walks with the seniors, do housework for them, or help them pay bills.

In the United States, there are many retirement communities. Seniors are living longer now, and they need nice places to live. In the early 1900s, the life expectancy[2] was 51 years old for women and 48 years old for men. Now the life expectancy for women is 81 and 76 for men.

Seniors in retirement communities want a comfortable life. The services and volunteers help the seniors a lot. Life in these communities can be cheerful and busy.

[1] retirement: when someone doesn't work anymore
[2] life expectancy: the average time people live.

B Mark the sentences *T* (true) or *F* (false).

_F_ 1. A retirement community does not offer services to seniors.

____ 2. Volunteers don't work with seniors in retirement communities.

____ 3. There aren't a lot of retirement communities in the U.S.

____ 4. Americans live longer now.

____ 5. The life expectancy for men was 48 in the early 1900s.

A Look at the pictures. Put the conversation in order.

_____ **Tony:** Good morning. Could I speak to Mr. Lewis, please?

_____ **Claire:** Goodbye.

_____ **Claire:** I'm sorry to hear that. I'll give him the message. I hope your daughter feels better soon.

_____ **Tony:** Yes, please. This is Tony. I am a salesclerk. I won't be in today. My daughter is sick, and I have to take her to the doctor.

__1__ **Claire:** Hello. Buy Smart Electronics. How can I help you?

_____ **Tony:** Thank you very much. Goodbye.

_____ **Claire:** He's not in yet. Can I take a message?

B Check all the different things you can do with your phone.

_____ use a GPS app   _____ text

_____ take videos   _____ take photos

_____ read books   _____ make international calls

_____ get a cab   _____ play games

_____ play music   _____ pay someone

C List two other things you can do with your phone:

1. _____

2. _____

UNIT 7 — What's for Dinner?

LESSON 1 VOCABULARY

A Look at the pictures. Match the words with the pictures. Use the words in the box.

| jar | bunch | carton | box | can | bottle | bag | ~~package~~ | loaf | six-pack |

1. _package_   2. _____   3. _____   4. _____   5. _____

6. _____   7. _____   8. _____   9. _____   10. _____

B Complete the conversation. Use the words in A.

Dina: Hi, Cesar. Would you like me to cook that ____box____ of spaghetti for dinner?
1

Cesar: That's a good idea. I'll open a _____ of spaghetti sauce for you. What
2
about a drink?

Dina: That would be nice. Can I have a _____ of soda?
3

Cesar: Sure. What about that _____ of bread and that _____ of grapes?
4   5
Should we have them, too?

Dina: OK. We have a _____ of ice cream. Maybe we can have some after dinner.
6

Cesar: Well, I shouldn't eat any dessert tonight. I had some earlier.

A **Complete the paragraph. Use the words in the box.**

prices	unit prices	store brand	a problem
a lot of coupons	at saving money	~~like to spend a lot~~	supermarket flyers

Lisa and Adam don't _____*like to spend a lot*_____ of money on food.
<u>1</u>

How do they save money? First, they read the _____
<u>2</u>

and compare _____ at home. At the supermarket,
<u>3</u>

they check the _____ and buy store brands. They
<u>4</u>

also use _____.
<u>5</u>

Lisa and Adam are good _____ at the
<u>6</u>

supermarket, but sometimes they want a special kind of food, like ice cream.

This isn't _____. They just buy the
<u>7</u>

_____ because it's usually cheaper than a
<u>8</u>

name brand.

B **Look at the flyers. Then answer the questions. Use complete sentences.**

1. Which juice is a better buy, one gallon for $4.00 or a half gallon for $2.50?
   <u>One gallon for $4.00 is a better buy.</u>

2. Which cheese is a better buy, ten ounces for $3.95 or five ounces for $1.90?
   _____

3. Which ice cream is a better buy, two pints for $6.00 or one pint for $2.75?
   _____

4. Which bunch of grapes is a better buy, two bunches for $2.99 or one bunch
   for $1.75?
   _____

A Look at the pictures. Circle the count nouns and underline the noncount nouns.

1. (carrots)

2. butter

3. potatoes

4. salt

5. water

6. mushrooms

B Check (✓) *How many* or *How much*. Then complete the questions.

	How many	*How much*	Questions
1. tomatoes	✓		How many tomatoes do you have?
2. soda			_____ do you have?
3. flour			_____ do you have?
4. bananas			_____ do you have?

C Complete the questions. Use *How many* or *How much*.

1. A: _____How much_____ cheese do you want?

   B: I want eight ounces of cheese, please.

2. A: _____ oranges does she eat every day?

   B: She eats two oranges every day.

3. A: _____ cartons of milk do they have?

   B: They have two cartons of milk.

4. A: _____ juice does he drink a day?

   B: He drinks eight ounces of juice a day.

D Unscramble the sentences.

1. need / some / They / milk

   They need some milk.

2. doesn't / tomatoes / any / She / have

   _____

3. some / salt / There's / in the soup

   _____

4. He / any / cheese / eat / doesn't

   _____

5. want / oil / some / We

   _____

E Complete the conversations. Use *a, an, any, some, how many,* or *how much.*

1. **A:** Did you buy _____ some _____ milk?

   B: Yes, I did. There's _____ carton of milk in the refrigerator.

   A: Great! Can I have _____ milk for my coffee?

2. **A:** I'd like _____ eggs and _____ bread for breakfast, please.

   B: _____ eggs do you want? Do you want _____ jam, too?

   A: I want one egg, but I don't want _____ jam.

3. **A:** _____ olive oil do we have?

   B: We don't have _____ olive oil.

   A: Can you please buy _____ olive oil at the supermarket?

4. **A:** Are there _____ apples in the refrigerator?

   B: Yes, there are. _____ do you want?

A Put the conversation in the correct order.

_____ **Keiko:** OK, the dairy section. Thank you. Oh, and the sausages?

_____ **Clerk:** The yogurt is in the dairy section next to the milk.

_____ **Clerk:** Sausages? You can find them in the meat section.

_____ **Keiko:** That's everything I need. Thanks a lot.

__1__ **Keiko:** Excuse me. Where's the yogurt, please?

_____ **Clerk:** You're welcome.

B Where can you find these items? Match the food with the supermarket sections.

fruit and vegetables

sausages and chicken

cookies and bread

butter and milk

ice cream

__1__ produce   _____ frozen food   _____ meat   _____ dairy   _____ baked goods

C Match the food with the supermarket sections.

__c__ 1. mushrooms   a. meat

_____ 2. loaf of bread   b. beverages

_____ 3. soda   c. produce

_____ 4. turkey   d. baked goods

DO THE MATH Go to page 90.

A Read the article. What are some healthy foods?

A Healthy Diet for a Busy Lifestyle

YOUR HEALTH TODAY

Many people don't eat the right food because they are busy. They think it takes a lot of time to have a healthy diet, but that's not always true. Many healthy foods are quick and easy to prepare.

For example, put some cheese, tomatoes, and cold chicken on whole-grain bread. To add some calcium, eat some yogurt. This healthy lunch is ready in minutes.

Fruit and vegetables are also easy to eat. Take a bag of grapes, oranges, or apples to work or school. Cut some carrots and eat them. Don't forget, vegetable soup is always great on a cool day.

It's important to drink the right things too. Soda has a lot of sugar and calories, and drinking too many cups of coffee is not healthy. Drink milk, fruit juice, or water. Many doctors want people to drink eight cups of water every day!

On busy days, people can still have a healthy diet. It might be easy to open a bag of potato chips, but they are not healthy. Nuts are healthier than potato chips, and it's also easy to open a package of nuts! ■

B Mark the sentences *T* (true) or *F* (false). Change the false sentences. Make them true.

                  doesn't
_F_ 1. It takes a lot of time to eat healthy food.

____ 2. Yogurt doesn't have calcium.

____ 3. Grapes, oranges, and apples can be easy to eat.

____ 4. Potato chips are healthier than nuts.

____ 5. Busy people can have a healthy diet.

C Read the nutrition label. Write the questions.

1. _How many servings are in a box?_

   There are eight servings in a box.

2. _____

   One serving is two ounces.

3. _____

   There are 200 calories in one serving.

4. _____

   There are ten calories from fat in one serving.

Nutrition Facts		
Servings per box: 8		
Serving size: 2 oz		
Amount per serving		
Calories per serving:		200
Calories from fat:		10
		% Daily Value
Total fat 1g		2%
Saturated fat 0g		0%
Trans fat 0g		
Cholesterol 0mg		0%

A Circle the containers, weights, and measurements in the puzzle.

| quart | bunch | can | pint | pound | box | ~~ounces~~ | carton | loaf | bag |

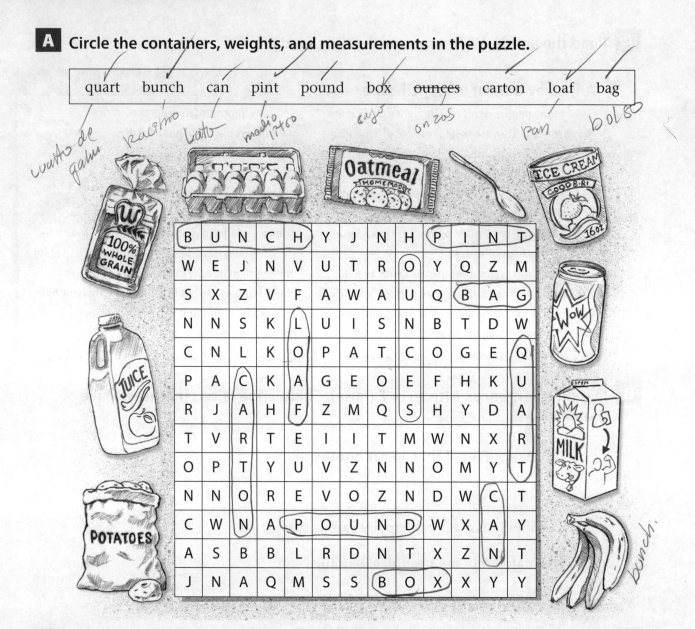

B Complete the chart. Use the words in the box.

a quart of juice	a bunch of bananas	~~16 ounces of chicken~~	a pint of ice cream
a pound of sausages	a box of cookies	a can of soda	a carton of milk
a loaf of bread	a bag of apples		

Meat	16 ounces of chicken
Dairy	
Drinks	
Produce	
Baked Goods	

LESSON 1 VOCABULARY

A Complete the sentences. Use the words in the box.

antihistamine	antacid	~~cough syrup~~	recommend
antibiotic ointment	eardrops	pain reliever	pharmacists

1. Rasha is coughing a lot. Can she have some _____cough syrup_____?

2. Naomi is allergic to cats. Please give her an _____.

3. I have a bad headache. Do you have a _____?

4. Rico ate spicy food and has heartburn now. He wants to take an _____.

5. Antonia has an earache. She needs _____.

6. You should use some _____ for the cut on your hand.

7. _____ usually _____ an antihistamine for allergies.

B Look at the picture. Match the numbers in the picture with the sentences.

_3_ Alex has a rash.

_1_ Dan's ankle is swollen.

_2_ Midori is sneezing and has a runny nose.

_4_ Carlos has a fever.

_5_ Lisa is nauseous and dizzy.

_6_ Julie has a cough.

A **Look at the pictures. Complete the paragraphs. Use the words in the box.**

had a backache	gave him a filling	to the chiropractor
~~a bad toothache~~	made an appointment	have to rest

Nadim had a terrible day yesterday. In the morning, he woke up with

_____a bad toothache_____. He called in sick, and then he _____
      1   2

to see the dentist. At the appointment, the dentist _____.
                                                                            3

In the afternoon, Nadim hurt his back. He _____. He went
                                                                   4

_____. The chiropractor said, "You _____ for
            5   6

a few days."

That night, Nadim went to bed and tried to forget about his day.

B **Complete the conversation. Use the words in the box.**

see his doctor	~~make an appointment~~	Could you make
That's good	the problem	about 11:30

A: Good morning. I need to ___make an appointment___ for my son. He needs
                                                  1

   to _____.
                  2

B: What's _____?
                        3

A: Well, he has a terrible cough, and he has a fever.

B: How _____ this morning?
                        4

A: My son is very sick. _____ it earlier?
                                              5

B: How about 9:30?

A: _____. Thank you very much!
            6

A **Complete the sentences. Use the simple past and the verbs in parentheses.**

1. Mei _____fell_____ off her bicycle and _____hurt_____ her back. (fall, hurt)

2. James _____ his finger and it _____ a lot. (cut, bleed)

3. She _____ her leg in a car accident. (break)

4. Martin _____ his hand at work yesterday. (burn)

5. They _____ sick after dinner last night. (feel)

6. Patricia _____ a toothache yesterday. (have)

7. We _____ to the hospital very quickly when we heard about the accident. (get)

8. Marina _____ down the stairs and _____ her ankle. (fall, sprain)

B **Unscramble the sentences. Use the simple past.**

1. Nancy / at 9:00 p.m. / fall asleep / last night
   Nancy fell asleep at 9:00 p.m. last night.

2. The children / last summer / every night / play soccer
   _____

3. Binita / yesterday morning / have a headache
   _____

4. Natasha and Boris / two years ago / fall in love
   _____

5. He / at work / last week / hurt his back
   _____

C **Match the questions with the answers.**

_c_ 1. When did he have a car accident?   a. She fell in the garage.

____ 2. Did she have a toothache yesterday?   b. Yes, he did.

____ 3. Did you cut your finger?   c. He had a car accident last year.

____ 4. Did he hurt his back?   d. Yes, I did.

____ 5. How did she break her leg?   e. No, she didn't.

D Look at the pictures. Complete the conversations. Use the words in the box.

hurt ~~Herir~~	fell off _cayó_	sprained _torcido_
~~burned~~	broke	burned _Quemado_

Lisa

1. **A:** What happened to Lisa?

   B: She ___burned___ her finger.

   A: How did she do that?

   B: She ___burned___ it on the stove.

Jung

2. **A:** What happened to Jung?

   B: He ___hurt___ his back.

   A: How did he do that?

   B: He ___fell off___ a ladder. _se cayo de una escalera_

Jack

3. **A:** What happened to Jack?

   B: He ___broke___ his arm.

   A: How did he do that?

   B: He ___sprained___ his ankle and fell on his arm.

E Complete the questions. Use the simple past and the verbs in parentheses.

1. **A:** Did _____ he have _____ an accident at work yesterday? (have)

   B: Yes, he did.

2. **A:** Why did _____ the party early? (leave)

   B: They were tired.

3. **A:** Did _____ to work yesterday? (drive)

   B: No, she took the bus.

4. **A:** How did _____ her arm? (break)

   B: She fell off her bike.

5. **A:** How did _____ his foot? (hurt)

   B: A big box fell on it.

A Complete the conversation. Use the words in the box.

| How often | ~~your prescription~~ | refill the prescription |
| times a day | for ten days | take more than |

Dr. Zakari: OK, Lina. Here is _____your prescription_____.
 1

Lina: _____ should I take the pills?
 2

Dr. Zakari: Three _____. Take one pill every eight hours.
 3

Don't _____ three pills a day.
 4

Lina: For how long?

Dr. Zakari: Take them _____. Then come back to see me. I might
 5

want you to _____.
 6

Lina: Thank you, Dr. Zakari.

B Read the prescription label. Mark the sentences _T_ (true) or _F_ (false).

__F__ 1. This prescription is for Dr. Chow.

_____ 2. This prescription is for shoulder pain.

_____ 3. Ali should eat food when he takes
a pill.

_____ 4. It's okay to take 10 pills a day.

_____ 5. Ali can refill the prescription until
December 2018.

> WT's Parmacy
> Ali Hala
> 822 Reddy Street
> Palo Alto, CA 94306
>
> Take 1 pill by mouth 2 times a day
> for shoulder pain. Take with meals.
> No more than 3 pills every 24 hours.
>
> **Refill: 2 Before 05/12/18**
> Prescription from: Dr. Chow

C Put the conversation in the correct order.

_____ **Pharmacist:** Your prescription is ready. You have to take two pills, two times a
day for 10 days.

_____ **Customer:** It's January 25, 1978.

_____ **Customer:** Do I really have to take them after meals?

_____ **Pharmacist:** Date of birth?

_____ **Customer:** Did you say two times a day?

_____ **Pharmacist:** Yes, it is very important.

__1__ **Customer:** I'd like to pick up my prescription please. My name is Lisa Robinson.

_____ **Pharmacist:** Yes, and take them after meals.

_____ **Customer:** OK. Thank you.

DO THE MATH Go to page 91.

A Read the article. What should you do first when there is an accident?

Accidents on the Job

Sometimes there are accidents in the workplace. What should you do when there is an accident at work? Here are three important rules to follow:

1. **Help injured employees immediately.** Get the first-aid kit, and use the supplies. In a serious emergency, call a doctor or emergency services.

2. **Write down all important information.** Who was injured? When and where did the accident happen? How did the accident happen?

3. **Complete an accident report for your supervisor.** Your supervisor has to know about the accident. It's important that the right people have all the forms they need. This helps the injured person get good medical treatment[1] now and in the future.

For accidents at work, know what to do before they happen. Find the first-aid kit, and check the supplies. Write down emergency telephone numbers. In the future, you will be ready and can help co-workers or yourself.

[1] medical treatment: help for an injured or sick person

B Mark the sentences *T* (true) or *F* (false).

__T__ 1. After an accident, the first step is to help any injured people.

____ 2. You always have to call emergency services when there's an accident.

____ 3. The supervisor needs to know about accidents at work.

____ 4. Find the first-aid kit immediately after an accident.

____ 5. An accident report doesn't help an injured person.

C Look at the first-aid supplies. Check (✓) the supplies you see.

✓ bandages   ____ gloves

____ thermometer   ____ antibiotic ointment

____ scissors   ____ antiseptic wipes

A **Complete the paragraph. Use the words in the box.**

Hinchado   *herido*

allergic	antihistamine	swollen	injured	fever
sneezing	~~antiseptic~~	runny	pain	bandage

Estornudor   *liquido*   *dolor*   *Vendaje*

The nurse at our company was very busy yesterday. First, Mr. Harris cut his finger.

The nurse cleaned it with an ___*antiseptic*___ wipe and put a ___*bandage*___ on it.
4-down 3-down

Then Ms. Jones came in. She had a ___*allergic*___ nose and was ___*sneezing*___
2-down 9-across

a lot. Ms. Jones was probably ___*swollen*___ to something, so the nurse gave her an
6-across

_____. Then Mr. Wilson came in. He felt hot. He had a ___*pain*___
4-across 8-across

and a headache. The nurse gave him a _____ reliever. Finally, Mr. Dodd came
1-down

in. He _____ his ankle when he fell on the stairs. It was _____, so
5-down 7-across

the nurse told him to rest. What a busy day!

B **Write the words in the puzzle. Use the information in A.**

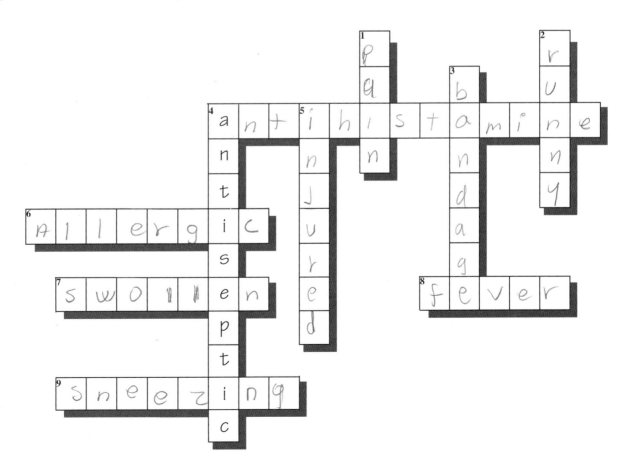

A Look at the bank statement. Complete the sentences. Use the words in the box.

~~bank statement~~	credit card bill	debit card
personal check	current balance	savings account

1. Every month Luisa gets a _____ bank statement _____ for her checking account.

2. Her _____ personal check _____ for this month is $2,000.50.

3. Luisa wrote a _____ to Oakwood Apartments.

4. Luisa used her _____ to withdraw $20.00.

5. Luisa transferred $100 to her _____ savings account _____

6. Luisa paid $250.50 for her _____ credit card bill.

STATE BANK   *Page 1 of 3*

Monthly statement

CHECKING ACCOUNT	CURRENT BALANCE
9876543	$2,000.50

DATE	TRANSACTION	AMOUNT
2/01	Oakwood Apt. rent—check #167	800.00
2/10	Internet payment— Star Energy	150.00
2/16	Deposit	500.00
2/18	Withdrawal—ATM	20.00
2/20	Transfer—savings account	100.00
2/20	Quest Credit— check #168	250.50

B Complete the sentences. Use the words in the box.

your PIN	enter the amount	remove your
~~insert your debit~~	take your cash	insert

1. First, _____ insert your debit _____ card for service.

2. Next, enter _____ your PIN _____.

3. For a deposit, _____ enter the amount _____ your cash or check.

4. For cash, first _____ you want to withdraw and press *Enter*.

5. Then _____ from the ATM.

6. Finally, don't forget to _____ debit card before you go.

A **Complete the paragraph. Use the words in the box.**

had a special offer	total budget	a great bargain	have picnics	cost $35.00
compare prices	picnic table	looked online	made a list	~~fix up~~

buy a picnic table

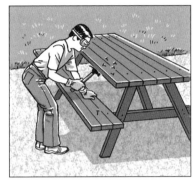
build a picnic table

have a picnic

Jun wanted to ___fix up___ a picnic area in his backyard. First, he _____ of
everything he needed. His _____ was $150.00. Next, he _____ for different
tables. After that, he went to different stores to _____. One store _____ on a
"Picnic Table in a Box." The table was only $100.00. That was _____. He bought
the _____, some paint, and some plants. The plants _____, and the paint cost
$15.00. Finally, Jun built and painted the table. Now Jun and his family can _____
in their backyard.

B **Read the paragraph. Complete the chart.**

Gabriela wants to fix up her new office, but she doesn't have a lot of money. She needs
a file cabinet, a new computer desk, a comfortable chair, and a picture for the wall. She
can spend $275. A co-worker wants to sell his file cabinet for $75. There's a desk on sale for
$80 at a store near Gabriela's house. She also saw a chair in a newspaper flyer. It costs $65.
Gabriela still has money for a picture. How much money can she spend on the picture?

Gabriela's new office	Amount
file cabinet	$75
computer desk	
comfortable chair	
picture for the wall	
Total budget: $275	

A Match the parts of the sentences.

__d__ 1. Joe bought some stamps to   a. she wanted to exercise.

____ 2. Sasha bought eardrops because   b. buy a pain reliever.

____ 3. Paula went to the park because   c. she had an earache.

____ 4. Jeff went to the pharmacy to   d. mail some letters.

B Complete the sentences. Write *it, they,* or *X.* (*X* = nothing)

1. Pablo wrote a personal check to _____X_____ pay his credit card bill.

2. The photocopier broke because _____ was old.

3. Ana and Rita got their GED certificates because _____ wanted better jobs.

4. Adam needs more work experience to _____ apply for that job.

5. Yoshi likes his apartment because _____ is in a safe neighborhood.

6. Carol bought three packages of cookies because _____ were on sale.

C Answer the questions. Use *to* or *because* and the words in parentheses.

to + verb

1. **A:** Why did Yasmin go to the hospital? (visit her mother)

   B: _She went to the hospital to visit her mother._

2. **A:** Why did Mario go to the bank? (deposit a check)

   B: _____

3. **A:** Why did Sue go to the library? (return some books)

   B: _____

because

4. **A:** Why did Mario go to the ATM? (needed some cash)

   B: _____

5. **A:** Why did James go to the baseball game? (had tickets)

   B: _____

6. **A:** Why did Oko and Paul go to the supermarket? (wanted some sugar)

   B: _____

D Look at the pictures. Complete the sentences. Use the words in the box.

to refill a prescription	wanted some books
~~wanted a bachelor's degree~~	to withdraw some cash

1. Franco went to school because he
   <u>wanted a bachelor's degree.</u>

3. Tom went to the pharmacy
   <u>to refill a prescription.</u>

2. Wendy went to the bank
   <u>to withdraw some cash.</u>

4. Min went to the library because she
   <u>wanted some books.</u>

E Read the questions. Write answers with *to* or *because*. Use your own ideas.

1. Why do people use debit cards?

   They use debit cards _____

2. Why do people go to home-improvement stores?

   They go to home-improvement stores _____

3. Why do people study English?

   They study English _____

F Use *too* or *enough* and the word in parentheses to write sentences.

1. This table is too expensive. (cheap)
   <u>It is not cheap enough.</u>

2. The apartment is not big enough. (small)

   _____

3. These pants are too short. (long)

   _____

4. The desk is not high enough. (low)

   _____

A **Put the conversation in the correct order.**

_____ **Customer:** Because it's too big. I need a smaller one. Here's my receipt.

_____ **Customer:** I'd like to exchange it, please.

__1__ **Customer:** Good morning. I would like to return this shirt.

_____ **Clerk:** Would you like a refund, or do you want to exchange the shirt?

_____ **Clerk:** OK. Why are you returning it?

B **Complete the conversation. Use the sentences in the box.**

You can't get a refund without a receipt.	Because I don't like the color.
I'll exchange it for a different color.	Why are you returning it?
~~I'd like to return this sweater.~~	I don't have it.

Jane: Excuse me. _I'd like to return this sweater._
                                              1

Clerk: That's fine. _____
                                    2

Jane: _____
              3

Clerk: OK. Do you have your receipt?

Jane: Yes, I think so. Oh, no! _____
                                                    4

Clerk: I'm sorry. _____ Would you like to
                              5
exchange it?

Jane: OK. _____
                        6

C **Match the questions with the answers.**

__c__ 1. Why are you returning the shoes?   a. Yes, I do. Here it is.

_____ 2. Do you have your receipt?   b. Sure. Here are some smaller shirts.

_____ 3. Would you like a refund?   c. They are too big for me.

_____ 4. Would you like to exchange this?   d. Yes, I would. How much is it?

_____ 5. Can I exchange this shirt for a smaller one?   e. No, I'd like a refund, please.

DO THE MATH Go to page 92.

A Read the article. What should you do when your credit card is stolen?

Stolen Credit Card?
What to Do

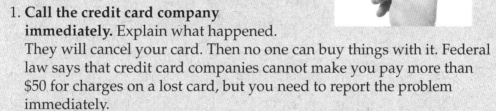

Did someone take your card? If yes, this is what you should do:

1. **Call the credit card company immediately.** Explain what happened. They will cancel your card. Then no one can buy things with it. Federal law says that credit card companies cannot make you pay more than $50 for charges on a lost card, but you need to report the problem immediately.

2. **Check your credit card bill.** Look at your next credit card bill carefully. Are there problems? Check each transaction carefully and call the credit card company if there are any problems.

The credit card company will usually send you a new card quickly. Protect your new card and keep the credit card company's phone number in a safe place. Make sure you keep a record of all your credit cards and their information. Then it will be easier to report any problems in the future.

B Answer the questions. Use complete sentences.

1. When should you report a missing credit card?

   You should report a missing credit card immediately.

2. What will your credit card company do when you report a missing card?

   _____

3. What can happen if you don't report the problem immediately?

   _____

4. Why should you look at your next credit card bill?

   _____

5. What should you do to make it easier to report any problems in the future?

   _____

A Circle the words in the puzzle.

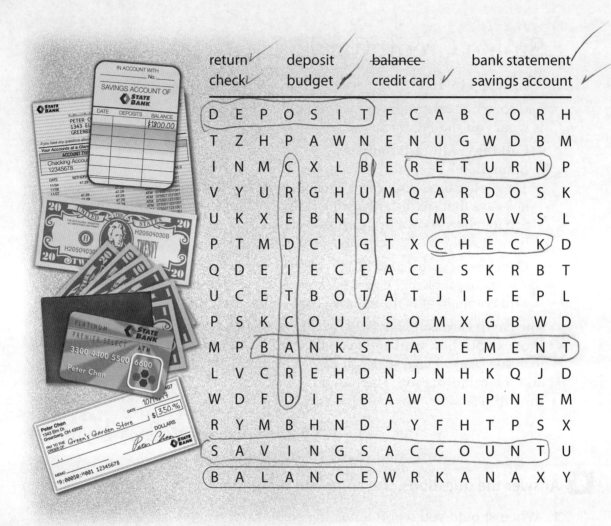

return   deposit   ~~balance~~   bank statement
check   budget   credit card   savings account

```
D E P O S I T F C A B C O R H
T Z H P A W N E N U G W D B M
I N M C X L B E R E T U R N P
V Y U R G H U M Q A R D O S K
U K X E B N D E C M R V V S L
P T M D C I G T X C H E C K D
Q D E I E C E A C L S K R B T
U C E T B O T A T J I F E P L
P S K C O U I S O M X G B W D
M P B A N K S T A T E M E N T
L V C R E H D N J N H K Q J D
W D F D I F B A W O I P N E M
R Y M B H N D J Y F H T P S X
S A V I N G S A C C O U N T U
B A L A N C E W R K A N A X Y
```

B Complete the sentences. Use the words in A.

1. Fernando always knows the current _____ balance _____ in his checking account.

2. Gabriela has $5,000 in her _____.

3. Alan got a new shirt from his sister, but it's too small. He wants to _____ it.

4. Every month we _____ $500 in our checking account.

5. Julio has personal checks, a debit card, and one _____.

6. Ali always checks his _____ carefully.

7. Sara has to write a _____ for her rent every month.

8. Sue wants to fix up her bathroom. Her _____ is $200.

A Match the pictures with the words.

 1 PERMANENT RESIDENT CARD

 2

 3

What is the 4th of July?

 4

 5 PASSPORT United States of America

_4_ take an oath of allegiance

_3_ take a citizenship test

_5_ get a passport

_2_ fill out an application for naturalization

_1_ get a green card

B Complete the chart. Use the words in the box.

~~Congress~~	governor	city council	president	U.S. representative
U.S. senator	vice president	lieutenant governor	mayor	City Hall
White House	State House			

Federal Government	State Government	Local Government
Congress		

A Complete the paragraph. Use the words in the box.

decided to do	doesn't have enough	to raise money	help clean the park
~~went to a meeting~~	Grant Park is dirty	had an idea	people at the meeting

David and Angela live in a small town. One evening, they _____went to a meeting_____
1

of their neighborhood association. The _____ discussed many
2

community issues. For example, one problem was that _____. The
3

town _____ money to clean it. Angela _____.
4   5

She said, "Let's ask volunteers from the neighborhood to help." At the meeting they

_____ two things:
6

1. have a book sale _____ for the park,
7

2. ask people in the neighborhood to _____.
8

The plan worked. Now the park is clean, and everyone in the neighborhood can use it.

B Read the flyer. Answer the questions. Use complete sentences.

1. What's happening on June 10th?

   _There will be a book sale._____

2. What's the date for the park cleanup?

   _____

3. What time does it start?

   _____

4. Do the volunteers need to buy lunch?

   _____

5. Who do you call for more information?

   _____

> ## Grant Park
> ## Cleanup Project!
>
> ***Book Sale to raise money**
> Date: Saturday, June 10th
> Time: 10 a.m. to 4 p.m.
> Place: Grant Street School
>
> ***Park cleanup day**
> We will provide lunch for everyone!
> Date: Saturday, June 17th
> Time: 10 a.m. to 5 p.m.
> ❀ ❀ ❀
> For more information call:
> Angela Banks (215) 555-4392

A Look at the train rules. Complete the sentences with *must* or *must not*.

Rules on the train

1. You _____ must _____ sign your train ticket.
2. You _____ *must not* _____ play a radio on the train.
3. You _____ *must not* _____ smoke inside the train.
4. You _____ *must* _____ throw away trash.
5. You _____ *must not* _____ run in the aisles.
6. You _____ *must* _____ wear shoes on the train.

B Mark the sentences *T* (true) or *F* (false). Change the false sentences. Make them true.

_F_ 1. You must ^*not* use a cell phone.

____ 2. You must fasten your seat belt.

____ 3. You must not arrive on time.

____ 4. You must not smoke in the bathroom.

____ 5. You must put your feet in the aisle.

Rules on the airplane
Arrive on time.
Fasten your seat belt.
Don't smoke in the bathroom.
No cell phones.
Don't put your feet in the aisle.

C Complete the sentences. Use *must* or *must not*.

1. In a restaurant, you _____ must _____ pay for your food.
   You _____ run.

2. On a bus, you _____ play your radio too loud.
   You _____ stand behind the yellow line.

3. Pedestrians _____ walk in the street.
   They _____ wait for the walk signal.

4. In a car, you _____ wear a seat belt.
   You _____ drive on the sidewalk.

D Read the paragraphs. Circle the correct words.

I work in a big city park. My job is to help people

enjoy their time in the park. There are lots of things

people can do in the park. There are also rules. For

example, you (can /(must)) jog or walk on the park trails.
                         1
You (shouldn't / might not) hurt any of the animals
                  2
in the park, and you (must not / should) walk on the
                           3
flowers.

The park closes at 11 p.m. every day, so you

(can / must not) come into the park after that time.
       4
Sometimes, people ask me, "(Can / Must) I jog in the park
                                5
after 9 p.m.?" I say, "Well, you (can / must), but I don't
                                      6
think you (should / might). It (might not / must not) be
             7   8
safe." I really like to help people, so I like my job a lot!

E Complete the sentences with *must always* or *must never*.

1. Drivers ___ must always ___ stop when they see a train coming.

2. Cyclists _____ ride their bikes on the highway.

3. In a car, you _____ wear a seat belt.

4. Pedestrians _____ wait for the walk signal to cross the street.

LESSON 4 EVERYDAY CONVERSATION

A Complete the conversation. Use the words in the box.

photo ID	take care of it	photo is
~~Good morning~~	I see	it is

Security guard: _____Good morning_____.
1

May _____ your
2

_____, please?
3

Mario: Sure. Here _____.
4

Security guard: Did you know that your

_____ too old?
5

Mario: No, I'm sorry. I'll

_____
6

right away.

Security guard: OK. Have a good day.

B Match the questions with the answers.

__d__ 1. May I see your license and
registration, please?

____ 2. Did you know that your right
taillight is broken?

____ 3. May I see your transit pass?

____ 4. You must not speed on this street.

a. No, I didn't. I'll take care of it
right away.

b. I'm sorry, officer. I'll slow down.

c. I don't have one. It expired last week.

d. Sure officer. Here they are.

C Complete the sentences. Circle the correct words.

1. You (must /(should)) wear a sweater. It is cold outside.

2. You (must not / should not) go over the speed limit.

3. They (must / should) wear a seatbelt.

4. You (must / should) check your car engine regularly.

5. You (must / should) have a passport to travel to a foreign country.

6. We (must not / should not) play loud music in the car.

A Read about the U.S. Congress. What are the two parts of the U.S. Congress?

The U.S. Congress

There are two parts of the U.S. Congress: the Senate and the House of Representatives. What's the difference between these two parts?

The Senate

There are 100 senators in the Senate. There are two senators for each of the 50 states. Senators are elected, and being a senator is a full-time job. The job is for a term of six years. After this six-year term, senators can be reelected[1]. To be a senator, you must:
★ be at least 30 years old,
★ be a citizen of the United States for at least nine years, and
★ be a resident[2] of the state where you're elected.

The House of Representatives

There are 435 representatives in the House of Representatives. Representatives are elected, and this is a full-time job for them too. The job is for a term of two years. After this two-year term, representatives can be reelected. The number of representatives is different for each state. States with large populations have more representatives than states with small populations. To be a representative, you must:
★ be at least 25 years old,
★ be a citizen of the United States for at least seven years, and
★ be a resident of the state where you're elected.

[1] reelected: elected again
[2] resident: person who lives somewhere

B Mark the sentences *T* (true) or *F* (false). Change the false sentences. Make them true.

__T__ 1. There are 100 senators in the Senate.

____ 2. There are 335 representatives in the House of Representatives.

____ 3. You must be at least 25 years old to be a senator.

____ 4. The president chooses senators and representatives.

____ 5. Senators and representatives can be reelected.

____ 6. You don't have to be a U.S. citizen to be in Congress.

A Complete the sentences. Use the words in the box.

| speeding | application | license | test | council |
| vice | federal | oath | Senate | |

1. Who is the _____vice_____ president of the United States?
2. To become a citizen, you must take an _____ of allegiance.
3. Did you complete your _____ for naturalization?
4. The mayor and city _____ meet every month.
5. May I see your _____ and registration, please?
6. Did you pass the citizenship _____?
7. Slow down! You're really _____!
8. The U.S. Congress has two parts: the _____ and the House of Representatives.
9. Congress is part of the _____ government.

B Complete the puzzle. Use the words in A.

1. (v) _i_ _c_ _e_
2.
3.
4.
5.
6.
7.
8.
9.

C Write the circled letters from the puzzle in B. Answer the question.

How can you help your community?

____ ____ ____ ____ ____ ____ ____ ____ ____!
 1   2   3   4   5   6   7   8   9

A Complete the sentences. Use the words in the box.

power outage   vandalism   ~~accident~~   robbery   explosion   mugging

1. The traffic was heavy because there was an ___accident___ on the highway.

2. You could hear the _____ at the factory from far away.

3. The _____ victim was injured. Someone hit her and took her money.

4. It was very dark. There was a _____ in the apartment building.

5. There was a _____ at the bank. The robbers stole $1,000.

6. There was some _____ in my community. There are a lot of broken windows.

B Match the pictures with the sentences.

___d__ 1. Wildfires are common in the summer.

_____ 2. Volcanic eruptions can happen at any time.

_____ 3. Hurricanes have winds of 74 miles per hour or more.

_____ 4. It's dangerous to drive in a flood.

_____ 5. You can see a tornado coming toward you.

_____ 6. After the blizzard, there were three feet of snow on the ground.

A Rewrite the paragraph. Begin each sentence with a capital letter. End each sentence with a period. Use capital letters for names.

steve and nancy were driving home at 8 o'clock last night on the corner of grant avenue and park street they saw an accident there was smoke coming out of the car they saw a young man in the car steve called 911 on his cell phone an ambulance and a fire truck arrived in five minutes the man in the car was not hurt the firefighters saved him

Steve and Nancy were driving home at 8 o'clock last night. On the corner of

_____

_____

_____

_____

_____

_____

_____

_____

_____

_____

B Look at A. Mark the sentences *T* (true) or *F* (false).

_F_ 1. Steve and Nancy were driving to the airport.

____ 2. There was a young man inside the car.

____ 3. Steve called 911 for help.

____ 4. One person was hurt.

C Read the paragraph. Then complete the emergency report.

Paul Smith and his two sons returned home yesterday and saw that something was wrong! The front door of their house at 522 Lane Avenue was open. The TV and the computer were not in the house. Paul immediately called 911 to report a robbery. They waited outside for the police.

Emergency Report

Name: _____

Emergency: _____

Place: _____

A **Complete the sentences. Use the past continuous of the verbs in parentheses.**

1. It __wasn't raining__ when the accident happened. (not rain)

2. They _____ TV when there was a power outage. (not watch)

3. Mia _____ when her son arrived. (not sleep)

4. We _____ lunch when we heard the explosion. (not have)

5. Abdula _____ English when his sister started crying. (study)

6. My friends _____ soccer when the police arrived. (play)

7. Roger _____ to work when it started raining heavily. (drive)

8. Denise _____ at her desk when she felt the earthquake. (sit)

9. George _____ dinner when the blizzard started. (make)

10. Tomoko _____ her homework when her father called. (do)

B **Complete the conversation. Use the simple past or past continuous of the verbs in parentheses.**

Ron: Hi Jose. I have to tell you about an emergency I _____saw_____
1
yesterday. (see)

Jose: Really? What _____? (happen)
2

Ron: Well, I _____ to my car when I _____
3   4
a bank robbery. (walk, see)

Jose: _____ you call 911? (do)
5

Ron: Yes, I _____ 911 immediately. (call) The operator
6
_____ me some questions. (ask) Then she said, "The police
7
will be there in five minutes."

Jose: Did the police really arrive in five minutes?

Ron: Yes, they _____. (do) When they _____,
8   9
the robber _____ away in his car. (arrive, drive)
10

Jose: What happened next?

Ron: I don't know. I was late for work, so I _____! (leave)
11

C Read the story. Circle the correct forms of the verbs.

Cristina and her daughter Adriana are from Peru.
They (were visiting /(visited)) their family there last
summer. They (were leaving / left) for Lima in June.
When they (arrived / were arriving) at the airport,
Cristina's father and mother (waited / were waiting)
for them.

Cristina and Adriana (enjoyed / were enjoying)
their time in Peru. They (were going / went) to the
city of Cuzco and visited the famous ruins in Machu Picchu. Everyone (took / was taking)
pictures. One man (played / was playing) a flute. The music was beautiful.

Cristina and Adriana (had / are having) a good time in Peru last summer. They
(made / are making) plans for their trip for next year!

D Answer the questions about Cristina and Adriana. Use the information in A. Use complete sentences.

1. When did Cristina and Adriana visit their family?

   They visited their family last summer.

2. Where did they go?

   _____

3. Who was waiting for them at the airport?

   _____

4. What was everyone doing at Machu Picchu?

   _____

5. What was one man doing at Machu Picchu?

   _____

E Match the questions with the answers.

_b_ 1. What was he doing when you arrived?   a. He took the bus.

___ 2. How did he get to work?   b. He was watching TV.

___ 3. What time did they leave?   c. We drove to the movie theater.

___ 4. How did you get to the movie theater?   d. They were sleeping.

___ 5. What were the children doing?   e. They left at 6:00 p.m.

A Complete the conversation. Use the words in the box.

2201 Beverly Hills Road	(914) 555-0602	~~the emergency~~
What happened	fire truck	

911: 911. What's _____the emergency_____?
                                    1
Mei: It's a fire emergency.

911: _____?
                            2
Mei: I left a pot on the stove.

911: What is your address?

Mei: It's _____.
                            3
911: What number are you calling from?

Mei: _____. What should I do?
                            4
911: Leave the house immediately, and wait for the _____.
                                                                5

B Look at the graphs. Answer the questions.

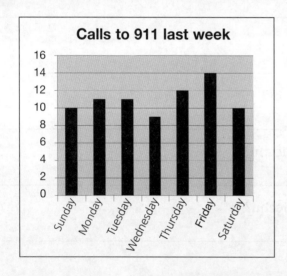

Calls to 911 last week

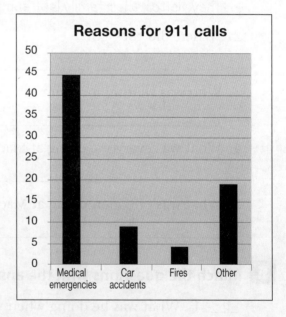

Reasons for 911 calls

1. Which day had more calls, Friday or Saturday? _____Friday_____

2. Which day had only nine calls? _____

3. How many calls were there during the week? _____

4. How many calls were there for a medical emergency? _____

5. Which reason was more common, fires or car accidents? _____

DO THE MATH Go to page 93.

A Read the brochure. What can you do to protect your home?

Protect Your Home

Do you want to make your home safe?
Here are a few things you can do to protect your home.

1. Make it difficult for strangers to come into your home. Buy good locks for your doors. A robber will often leave if it's difficult to get into your home.

2. Make sure you know your neighbors. They can call 911 for you, and you can do the same for them.

3. Have a lot of lights around your house. Use motion lights[1] outside. They help other people see robbers.

4. Get an alarm. It will make a loud sound when a robber opens your door.

Remember: Be safe and be prepared.
Call for help if you feel unsafe.

[1]**motion lights:** lights that turn on when someone moves near them

B Complete the sentences. Use words from the brochure in A.

1. You should make your house __difficult__ to enter.

2. It's a good idea to know your _____.

3. _____ lights will help other people see robbers.

4. An _____ will make a loud sound.

5. These ideas will protect your home from a _____.

Look at the pictures. Complete the crossword puzzle.

Across   Down

1.    9.    2.    7.

4.    10.    3. 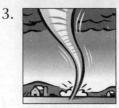   8.

6.    12.    5.    11.

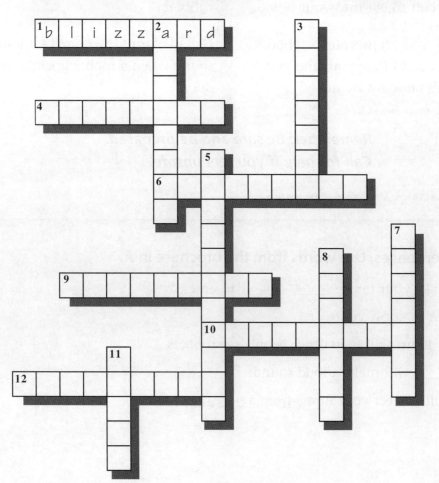

UNIT 12 Take the Day Off

LESSON 1 VOCABULARY

A Match the pictures with the sentences.

_____ Paula likes to go biking in September.

__1__ David likes to go camping in April.

_____ Tom sometimes goes fishing in August.

_____ Lucy usually goes hiking in May.

_____ Simon always goes skating in November.

B Look at the pictures. Match the parts of the sentences.

_a_ 1. *The Adventure Boys* is an   a. action computer game.

____ 2. *The Longest Nightmare* is a   b. romance movie.

____ 3. *Trip to the Stars* is a   c. horror movie.

____ 4. *Love in August* is a   d. science fiction movie.

____ 5. *The Stolen Notebook* is a   e. mystery book.

A Read the sentences. Put the sentences in the correct order. Then use the sentences to write the paragraph.

☐ On Thursday, Angela and her family are going to go to the zoo.

1̄ ~~Next weekend is a four-day weekend.~~

☐ They are going to visit the museum on Saturday afternoon.

☐ On Friday, they want to see *The Stolen Notebook*.

☐ Her children want to watch a soccer game on TV on Saturday evening.

☐ On Sunday afternoon, they are going to go to a concert in the park.

Next weekend is a four-day weekend.

_____

_____

_____

_____

_____

_____

B Read the newspaper ad. Answer the questions.

1. When does the first show for *Lady Blue* start?
   It starts at 12:35.

2. When does the last show for *Found in Chicago* start?

   _____

3. How much is a ticket for a child under the age of 12?

   _____

4. How much is a ticket for a 66-year-old adult?

   _____

5. Alan wants to see *Lady Blue* at 3:15. He is 45 years old. How much is his ticket?

   _____

Movie Studio 400

The Stolen Notebook
1:50, 4:20, 7:50, 10:00

Found in Chicago
2:35, 5:45, 8:30

Lady Blue
12:35, 3:15, 6:20, 9:40

Children under the age of 12 – $7.50
Adults – $14.00
Seniors over 65 – $10.00

Special discount today!

$4.00 off all shows before 4 p.m.!

A Complete the chart. Write the correct forms of the adjectives.

Adjective	Comparative	Superlative
1. funny	funnier	the funniest
2.	sadder	
3. large		
4.		the most exciting
5.	scarier	
6.		the best
7.	worse	
8. famous		
9.		the longest
10. popular		

B Complete the questions and answers. Use the superlative of the adjectives in parentheses.

1. **A:** What was _____the longest_____ movie this year? (long)

   B: *Found in Chicago* _____was the longest movie this year_____.

2. **A:** What was _____ movie this year? (good)

   B: *Lady Blue* _____.

3. **A:** Who was _____ actress in the movie? (famous)

   B: Jane Smith _____.

4. **A:** What was _____ movie this year? (bad)

   B: *Monsters and Elephants* _____.

5. **A:** What was _____ movie last year? (exciting)

   B: *Darkness* _____.

6. **A:** What was _____ movie this year? (funny)

   B: *Clown Time* _____.

C Read the list. Complete the questions. Then write the answers. Use the superlative.

1. What's _____the cheapest_____ Sunday activity?

   The cheapest Sunday activity is a free concert in

   the park.

2. What's _____ restaurant?

   _____

   _____

3. What's _____ movie?

   _____

   _____

4. What's _____ museum?

   _____

   _____

> Sue's List for This Week
>
> **The Most and the Best in Our Town**
>
> Cheap Sunday activity:
>
> Free concert in the park
>
> Interesting museum:
>
> The Science Museum
>
> Good restaurant:
>
> Max's Kitchen
>
> Funny movie:
>
> The Clowns

D Complete the sentences. Use the simple, comparative, and superlative forms of adjectives in parentheses.

1. (popular)

   Be Happy _____is a popular_____ book.

   Be Rich _____is more popular_____ than Be Happy.

   Live to Be 100 _____ book of all.

2. (bad)

   Happy Family _____ TV program.

   Party Time _____ than Happy Family.

   Lake Town _____ TV program of all.

3. (exciting)

   Basketball _____ sport.

   Football _____ than basketball.

   Soccer _____ sport of all.

A Complete the conversation. Use the words in the box.

most exciting	the greatest actors	~~was it~~
don't like romance	you think of it	did you do

A: I heard you went to the basketball game last Saturday. How _____was it_____?
1

B: Great! It was the _____ game this season.
2

How about you? What _____?
3

A: My wife and I saw that new movie, *Lady Blue*.

B: What did _____?
4

A: Frank Davis was great. He's probably one of _____ in
5

movies today.

B: Really?

A: But I _____ movies.
6

B: Yeah, I understand.

B Put the conversation in the correct order.

____ **Joe:** I agree. I saw the concert last month.

____ **Ellen:** On Sunday, we tried the new restaurant in town and then we went to the movies. The new place's food was terrible.

_1_ **Joe:** Hi Ellen, what did you do last weekend?

____ **Ellen:** On Saturday evening, we went to the soccer game. It was the most exciting game of the season.

____ **Joe:** Oh, I am sorry to hear about the new restaurant. Did you see the movie *The Stolen Notebook*? I thought it was fantastic!

____ **Joe:** I think so too! I saw the game on TV. The best one yet!

____ **Ellen:** On Saturday afternoon, my husband and I went to the concert in the park. It was amazing!

____ **Ellen:** Me too. It certainly is a great movie. I want to see it again!

A Read the online article. How can you prepare for a road trip?

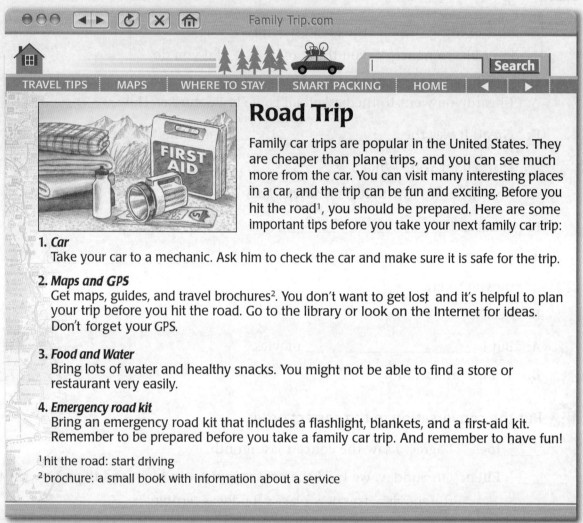

Family Trip.com

TRAVEL TIPS | MAPS | WHERE TO STAY | SMART PACKING | HOME

Road Trip

Family car trips are popular in the United States. They are cheaper than plane trips, and you can see much more from the car. You can visit many interesting places in a car, and the trip can be fun and exciting. Before you hit the road[1], you should be prepared. Here are some important tips before you take your next family car trip:

1. **Car**
   Take your car to a mechanic. Ask him to check the car and make sure it is safe for the trip.

2. **Maps and GPS**
   Get maps, guides, and travel brochures[2]. You don't want to get lost and it's helpful to plan your trip before you hit the road. Go to the library or look on the Internet for ideas. Don't forget your GPS.

3. **Food and Water**
   Bring lots of water and healthy snacks. You might not be able to find a store or restaurant very easily.

4. **Emergency road kit**
   Bring an emergency road kit that includes a flashlight, blankets, and a first-aid kit. Remember to be prepared before you take a family car trip. And remember to have fun!

[1] hit the road: start driving
[2] brochure: a small book with information about a service

B Answer the questions. Use complete sentences.

1. Why are family car trips popular in the United States?

   Family car trips are cheaper than plane trips, and you can see much more

   from a car.

2. What should your mechanic do before a car trip?

   _____

3. Why should you bring maps and a GPS?

   _____

4. Why should you bring water and snacks?

   _____

5. What should you have in your emergency road kit?

   _____

A There are over 18 words in the loop. Can you find them all? Write the words below.

computereducationalcomputeromanceexcitedoverestauranticketripicnicheaprogrammuseumovieexpensivexcitingoodangerouscienceducational

computer			
romance			

B How many words can you make using the letters in "educational program"?
Write as many words as you can. Each word must have three or more letters.

educational program

late			
map			

How many did you find?

10 words = ✶ Good work!
15 words = ✶✶ Great job!
20+ words = ✶✶✶ Excellent!

UNIT 1

Read the information. Then answer the questions.

1. There are 35 students in Ms. Smith's English class. Their first languages are Spanish, Japanese, Portuguese, and Arabic. Fifteen students speak Spanish. Ten students speak Japanese. Only two students speak Portuguese. How many students speak Arabic?

    _____

2. Ben and Molly are making flashcards. Ben is making 24 flashcards. Molly is making 15. How many flashcards are Ben and Molly making together?

    _____

3. Tomoko wants to be a nurse. Each class Tomoko takes is three credits. She takes five classes this semester. How many credits does she have this semester?

    _____

UNIT 2

A **Read the information. Then answer the question. Circle *a* or *b*.**

Charles can run 5 miles in 40 minutes. How long will it take him to run 15 miles?

a. 2½ hours

b. 2 hours

B **Read the information. Then answer the questions.**

Abdul can run 2 miles in 12 minutes. It is 4 miles from the bank to the post office. It is 3 miles from the post office to Abdul's apartment.

1. How long will it take Abdul to run from the bank to the post office?

    _____

2. How long will it take Abdul to run from the post office to his apartment?

    _____

UNIT 3

A Read the information. Then answer the question. Circle *a* or *b*.

Steve's rent is $500 a month. The security deposit is $200. How much will Steve spend on rent in one year including the deposit?

a. $6,000

b. $6,200

B Read the information about Lisa's rental agreement. Then answer the questions.

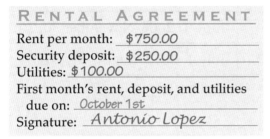

RENTAL AGREEMENT

Rent per month: $750.00

Security deposit: $250.00

Utilities: $100.00

First month's rent, deposit, and utilities
   due on: October 1st

Signature: Antonio Lopez

1. How much will Lisa pay on October 1st?

   _____

2. How much will she pay on November 1st?

   _____

3. How much will Lisa spend on rent and utilities from January to March? (Hint: Don't include the deposit.)

   _____

Answer the questions. Use the information in the chart.

Name	Job/Employer	Dates
Rita	Chef/Hotel Royale	January 1, 1990–December 31, 2016
George	Computer programmer/BZD, Inc.	March 1, 2011–September 30, 2015
Stan	Pilot/Concordia Airlines	April 1, 1999–May 31, 2016
Ahmed	Banker/B.N.A.T. Bank	February 1, 2004–October 31, 2017
Paola	Nurse/Brown Care Clinic	June 1, 2006–November 30, 2014
Ann	Office assistant/WAZ Industries	July 1, 2012–August 31, 2017

1. How long did Rita work as a chef at the Hotel Royale?

   She worked as a chef at the Hotel Royale for 27 years.

2. How long did George work as a computer programmer at BZD, Inc.?

   _____

3. How long did Stan work as a pilot at Concordia Airlines?

   _____

4. How long did Ahmed work as a banker at B.N.A.T. Bank?

   _____

5. How long did Paola work as a nurse at the Brown Care Clinic?

   _____

6. How long did Ann work as an office assistant at WAZ Industries?

   _____

Read about Daniel's new job. Then answer the questions.

Daniel started his new job last month. He works five days a week as a cashier at the gas station near his house. He makes $7.50 per hour. He works 40 hours a week. Last week, his boss asked him to work an extra two hours every day he works. He makes $12.00 per hour for every hour he works past his 40 hours. He is happy to be making some extra money to support his family.

1. How much does Daniel make per hour?

   _____

2. How much is his gross pay every week?

   _____

3. How much did he make extra last week?

   _____

4. How much did he make last week (40 hours + 10 extra hours)?

   _____

UNIT 6

Read the information. Then answer the questions. Circle _a_, _b_, or _c_.

1. Janet pays $24.00 for 4GB of data every month. How much does she pay for 6GB of data?

   a. $24.00

   b. $30.00

   c. $36.00

2. Jamal can send 1,500 text messages every month for $15.00. He has to pay $5.00 for 500 extra text messages. This month he sent 2,500 messages. How much is his bill this month?

   a. $25.00

   b. $15.00

   c. $20.00

3. Yoko bought a new phone for $650.00. She sold her old phone for $120.00. Her new phone company gave her $100.00 back. How much did Yoko pay out of her own money for her phone?

   a. $340.00

   b. $430.00

   c. $440.00

UNIT 7

Read the information. Then answer the questions. Circle *a, b,* or *c.*

1. Ali has $2.75 in his wallet. He wants to buy some sugar. One pound of sugar is $0.99. How much sugar can Ali buy?

    a. 2 pounds

    b. 3 pounds

    c. 4 pounds

2. Maria went to buy some milk, eggs, and bread. The milk was $3.50, the eggs were $5.20, and the bread was $2.99. She has a coupon and saved $0.60. How much did Maria spend?

    a. $11.19

    b. $10.99

    c. $11.09

3. Karen needs 3 cups of flour and 8 apples for her pie. She has 2 cups of flour and 10 apples at home. How much flour and how many apples does she need to buy?

    a. 1 cup of flour and 2 apples

    b. 1 cup of flour and no apples

    c. 2 cups of flour and 8 apples

UNIT 8

Read the information. Then answer the questions. Circle *a, b,* or *c.*

1. Lisa has some new medication. The bottle has 40 pills. She needs to refill it three more times. How many pills will she take in total?

    a. 120 pills

    b. 160 pills

    c. 200 pills

2. Every day, Wen took one pill after breakfast and one pill after dinner. After 45 days, the bottle was empty. How many pills did Wen take?

    a. 30 pills

    b. 60 pills

    c. 90 pills

3. Rosana has to take two pills two times a day for 45 days. She has enough pills for 30 days. How many pills does she have?

    a. 180 pills

    b. 140 pills

    c. 120 pills

4. The doctor told Brandy to take one pill two times a day for 60 days. She was confused and took two pills two times a day. After how many days was the bottle empty?

    a. 30

    b. 60

    c. 90

UNIT 9

Read the paragraph. Then answer the questions.

Luis went to the store and bought two shirts and two suits. The shirts cost $25.95 each, and the suits cost $280.00 each. He also bought a tie for $13.00. The next day, he returned one shirt and got a refund. Then he bought another tie.

1. How many shirts did Luis buy the first day?

   _____

2. How much money did Luis spend the first day?

   _____

3. How much was Luis' refund?

   _____

4. How many new shirts does Luis have in total?

   _____

5. How much did Luis spend on clothes in total?

   _____

UNIT 10

Complete the sentences. Write numbers for the words in parentheses.

This is a list of traffic violations in one year for one state in the United States.

1. The police gave _____ tickets for speeding. (one hundred thirty-nine thousand five hundred)

2. They stopped _____ people because they weren't wearing seat belts. (sixty-one thousand five hundred thirty-eight)

3. Police gave tickets to _____ people because they didn't stop at stop signs. (one thousand seven hundred twenty-five)

4. Police stopped _____ people because they weren't driving on the right side of the road. (two thousand one hundred eighty-four)

Read the graph. Then answer the questions.

CAUSES OF HOME ACCIDENTS

scissors	24,840
bags	54,004
bottles and jars	81,419
knives	381,354
stairs or steps	1,248,421

Source: Injury Facts 2015 Edition published by National Safety Council

1. What is the main cause of accidents in the home?

   _____

2. How many accidents were caused by scissors and bags?

   _____

3. Which caused more accidents, knives or scissors?

   _____

4. Which caused fewer accidents, bottles and jars or bags?

   _____

A Look at the ticket and read the information about the Wong family. Then answer the questions.

> ### ANNUAL COUNTY FAIR
> #### REGULAR ADMISSION
>
> ADULTS: $14.00   SENIORS OVER 60: $9.00
> CHILDREN UNDER 12: $7.00
>
> COME BEFORE 10 A.M.: ALL TICKETS ARE HALF PRICE!

Mr. and Mrs. Wong and their grandchildren, Kevin, Nancy, and Sue are planning to go to the County Fair this Sunday. Mr. Wong is 65, Mrs. Wong is 58, Kevin is 14, Nancy is 10, and Sue is 8 years old.

1. How much will the family spend at the County Fair for regular admission?

   _____

2. Mr. Wong says that the tickets are too expensive, so they arrive at the fair before 10:00 a.m. How much do the tickets cost?

   _____

B Read the information about science museum ticket prices. Answer the questions. Circle *a* or *b*.

1. Angela, her husband, and their two children, ages 8 and 10, are at the museum on Sunday. Which is the cheapest ticket?

   a. regular admission

   b. Family Day ticket

2. Simon and his two children, ages 12 and 16, are at the museum on Sunday. Which is the cheapest ticket?

   a. regular admission

   b. Family Day ticket

> **Science Museum**
> Regular Admission
> Adults: $12.00
> Seniors over 60: $8.00
> Children under 14: $6.00
> **Family Day ticket**
>   (Sunday only)
> Two adults and up to three
>   children under 14: $32.00